Casablanca Film Trivia: Here's Looking at You, Kid!

By

Tom Barnes

PUBLISHING
San Clemente, CA
© 2009

Casablanca Film Trivia

Papyrus Publishing
P.O. Box 3422
San Clemente, CA 92674-3422
1-888-846-1812

Although the author and publisher have made every effort to ensure the accuracy and completeness of information contained in this book, we assume no responsibility for errors, inaccuracies, omissions, or any inconsistency herein. Any slights of people, places, or organizations are unintentional.

First Printing 2008

ISBN No. 978-0-615-21579-2

Library of Congress Control Number: 2008932262

For ordering this book go to casablancatrivia.com
or write directly to Papyrus Publishing.

Typesetting and cover design by
CREST GRAPHIC DESIGN
661.255.6336

Printed in the United States by Delta Printing Solutions.

Attention Corporations, Universities, Colleges, High Schools, and Professional Organizations: Quantity discounts are available on bulk purchases of this book for educational, gift purposes, or as premiums for increasing magazine subscriptions or renewals. Special books or book excerpts can also be created to fit specific needs. For information, please contact Papyrus Publishing, P.O. Box 3422, San Clemente, CA 92674-3422, or go to casablancatrivia.com, or email casablancatrivia@cox.net

Dedication

*To all my students over the years
who have enjoyed playing the
"Casablanca Trivia Game,"
and to my wife Vonne
for her love and support.*

*Also, to the many fans of Casablanca,
may this book enhance your enjoyment
of this cultural icon.*

Table of Contents

Factoids

At the end of most chapters are interesting tidbits of information about the film. Many of these "factoids" provide information that can be helpful in answering the trivia questions. Others are just general information about the film.

The following are examples of representative factoids that are similar to the ones that appear in *Casablanca Film Trivia: Here's Looking at You, Kid!*

Factoid:

Casablanca is shot in 59 days and the budget is approximately $875,000.

Factoid:

The National Film Registry lists *Casablanca* as one of a select group of films deemed to be culturally, historically or aesthetically significant.

Factoid:

There are lots of drinks in *Casablanca* but only twice are people seen eating anything – Strasser and the German officers with their caviar the first night at Rick's Café, and Rick and Ilsa eating peanuts as they cruise on the *Seine* in the Paris flashback scene.

Factoid:

The reason that producer Hal Wallis chose Aeneas McKenzie, and his writing partner, Wally Kline to do the script from the play, McKenzie had the experience to deal with European characters and settings. The McKenzie/Kline script was never used.

Factoid:

Noted film critic Pauline Kael said about *Casablanca* that it is "A movie that demonstrates how entertaining a bad movie can be."

Factoid:

Casablanca cost $878,000 and came in about 8 percent over budget, primarily because Paul Henreid was held up for a month in finishing *Now Voyager,* which disrupted the shooting schedule.

Factoid:

Although he only worked for $1.12 an hour, the Warner Bros. story reader Stephen Karnot was the first person to recommend that a movie be made from the play "Everybody Comes to Rick's."

Factoid:

Julius Epstein, one of the many writers of *Casablanca*, said it had "a great deal of corn, more corn than was in the states of Kansas and Iowa combined."

Factoid:

Laszlo's character, greatly changed from the stage play from a playboy to a leader of the resistance, could have been modeled after Vojtech Pressig, an American of Czech nationality, who went underground after the German invasion and published an anti-Nazi, underground, newspaper called "*V boj*," until he was captured and sent to Dachau where he died in 1944.

Factoid:

The cut-out airplane at the final scene, is a Lockheed 12A Electra twin-engine transport plane; this type of plane was commonly exported from the United States in the late 1930s.

Factoid:

A primary reason why a new ending was not filmed when *Casablanca* received a negative review by a preview audience, is because Ingrid Bergman had already cut her hair for the role of Maria in *For Whom the Bell Tolls.*

Factoid:

A classic scene in *When Harry Met Sally,* has both Harry (Billy Crystal) and Sally (Meg Ryan) watching *Casablanca* on television, each from their own separate rooms.

Factoid:

The German headquarters in French Morocco is located at the posh Miramar Hotel, in the seaside resort town of Fedela, 24 miles from the Casablanca airport which itself is six miles from the center of Casablanca. Assuming he was coming from the German headquarters, Strasser arrived at the airport at break-neck speed.

Factoid:

In the scene when the Germans march into Paris, Ilsa is wearing a pinstriped suit and white blouse, not a blue dress.

Factoid:

Film critic Rick Corliss said that "*Casablanca* succeeds as allegory, popular myth, clinical psychology, or whatever, and as a superb romantic melodrama."

Factoid:

An avid anti-Nazi who made substantial financial contributions to the British and Allied war effort, Conrad Veidt, in playing Major Strasser said this about the role, "I know this man well. This role epitomizes the cruelty and criminal instincts and murderous trickery of the typical Nazi."

Factoid:

Director Rajeev Nath, who once thought about casting Paris Hilton as Mother Therese, is making a Bollywood remake of *Casablanca* called *Ezham Mudra (The Seventh Seal)* – that title is "ripped off" from the Ingmar Bergman classic 1959 film. To be set at a beachside restaurant in southern India, the storyline will feature the ethnic conflict in Sri Lanka between the Tamils and Sinahalese. Suresh Gopi will have Bogey's role and Mandira Bedi will have Ingrid Bergman's role.

Factoid:

Young French actress Michele Morgan was an early favorite for the role of Ilsa, but took herself out of the running by asking the exorbitant price of $55,000 which was more than twice what Ingrid Bergman was paid.

Factoid:

After the death of Humphrey Bogart in 1957, the start of the "*Casablanca* cult" and Bogart film festivals is launched by the Brattle Theatre in Cambridge, Massachusetts; where *Casablanca* is traditionally shown during Finals Week.

Factoid:

In the Warner Bros. cartoon parody of *Casablanca* called *Carrotblanca*, Bugs Bunny played Rick, Daffy Duck played Sam, and Tweety Bird played Renault.

Factoid:

There are six different animals either mentioned or seen in *Casablanca*: dog with an eye patch, monkeys, parrot, horses, fox, and hound.

Introduction

Casablanca Film Trivia: Here's Looking at You, Kid!

When it comes to describing the great American novel, experts and the common folk disagree; but in the greatest American film category, *Casablanca* wins hands down. *Citizen Kane, Gone With The Wind, The Godfather,* and *Star Wars* all have their fans, but no film rivals *Casablanca* as an accepted icon of popular culture. It is unique in the fact that it appeals to both the "filmaratti" and the "masses," something that the other contenders do not do.

Casablanca and I have grown up together. It went into general release a week after I was born, in January of 1943. I can't ever remember not loving *Casablanca*. One sultry August while in junior high school, I whiled away my time watching old movies all night long. *Casablanca* was one of my favorites. For the last 25 years of my 35-year high school teaching career, until I retired in 2005, I showed it to my history and social science classes, and we played a trivia board game (still in prototype stage) that I created based on the film. That board game is the basis for *Casablanca Film Trivia: Here's Looking at You, Kid!*

By turning 65 this year, the world's most revered film qualifies for Medicare, just like I do. Now that *Casablanca* has reached old age, it is time to reflect on the film's impact since winning the Academy Award for best picture 65 years ago. I say "winning" because that's what they used to say before the "politically correct" world changed it to "the Oscar goes to." What better way to honor *Casablanca* than a book of trivia about all aspects of the film and its filming. *Casablanca* deserves the 1130 questions that have been written about it.

Casablanca Film Trivia: Here's Looking at You, Kid! is divided into 33 chapters. Thirty-one of these chapters are each devoted to a specific category or theme – e.g. script & lines, drinks, geography, clothing and apparel, and critics. The final two chapters each have 100 questions; a potpourri of questions from a variety of categories, that are some of the most difficult questions in the book.

At the end of most of the chapters are "factoids," interesting bits of information about the film that can be helpful in answering some of the trivia questions. There are nearly a hundred of these factoids scattered throughout the book.

It is my hope that lovers of this film, and classic films in general, will enjoy the book. Watch the film, consult the books in the bibliography, and see how many questions you can answer about America's "best loved film – *Casablanca*."

Here's looking at you, kid!

Tom Barnes

2008

~ Notes ~

~ *Notes* ~

"... the fortunate ones through money, or influence, or luck, might obtain exit visas and scurry to Lisbon, and from Lisbon to the New World. But others wait in Casablanca, and wait, and wait, and wait."

~ Narrator ~

Chapter 1
Script & Lines

No single film has ever had more memorable and frequently quoted lines than *Casablanca*. With an Academy Award winning script written by Julius and Philip Epstein, Howard Koch, and others, the sharp dialogue has been one of the films most enduring features.

Questions:

1. What does Rick tell Ilsa we will always have, as he leaves her in the closing scene on the tarmac at the airport?

2. What toast does Rick say to Ilsa, both with and without a drink, four different times in the film?

3. Which character in the film says, "Play it again, Sam?"

4. Renault hypocritically says he is "shocked" by what activity that is going on at Rick's Café, as he collects his winnings while closing it down?

5. When Rick points his gun at Renault's heart, Renault says his heart is his _____ .

6. After Rick sends Yvonne home, Renault chides him for throwing away women because some day they may be _____ .

7. What does Rick sarcastically say his occupation is, when he is interrogated by Strasser the first night in the café?

8. In the closing scene at the airport, when Rick sends Ilsa away with Victor Laszlo, what does Rick say he is "no good at being," that he is actually "being" by this action?

9. In a perfunctory manner, what does Renault tell his officers to do a number of times in the film, when he sees a crime has been committed?

10. What does Rick say to Louis, that is the closing line of the film, and considered one of the classic closing lines in all cinema?

11. What two alliterative words does Rick use to describe his bar, when he gets drunk in his room after seeing Ilsa with Victor Laszlo earlier that evening?

12. What does Rick tell Ferrari he does not buy when he is offered money for Sam?

13. What reason does Ferrari give for Rick's shipment always being a little short?

14. The problems of three people doesn't amount to what according to Rick in the closing scene?

15. When Louis asks Rick why he came to Casablanca, and Rick tells him it was "for his health, for the waters," Louis incredulously says "What waters? We're in the desert." What was Rick's reply?

16. The first night in the café, Rick dismisses Yvonne with the same words Ilsa had said to Rick when he suggested that he and Ilsa get married in Marseilles. What are the words?

17. What are the last three words that Ilsa says to Rick as she walks to the plane in the closing scene? These are the same three words that she wrote on her note to Rick when she left him in Paris.

18. What *leitmotiv* refrain does Louis Renault tell the *gendarmes* to do after Major Strasser has been shot?

19. According to Rick, what is it that is a part of Victor's work, the thing that keeps him going?

20. What is Henri going to do with the champagne at *La Belle Aurora* before he will let the Germans drink any of it?

21. According to Renault, when he is first talking to Strasser, where does "everybody come to" in Casablanca? This is the name of the play on which the film is based.

22. After the tarmac scene when Victor and Ilsa leave, Louis says to Rick, "Well I was right, you are a _____ ."

23. Throughout the film what does Rick constantly say that he does for nobody, which is ironic because he actually does it for a number of people?

24. Because the case is so important, what does Renault tell Strasser he is doing to solve the murder of the German couriers?

25. What does Rick say for the last time on the tarmac to Ilsa, that he had said three other times in the film?

26. What slang word does Rick use to describe the type of "finish" of the guy standing on a station platform in Paris in the rain?

27. What kind of characters does the police officer say over the microphone in the opening scene, should be rounded up and searched?

28. Besides being a sentimentalist, what else does Louis say Rick has become at the airport scene?

29. What two names does Rick instruct Louis to fill in on the "Letters of Transit?"

30. Besides hearing very little, the English couple in the opening scene say they also _____ .

Answers:

1. **Paris**
2. **"Here's looking at you, kid"**
3. **No one. It is never said.**
4. **gambling**
5. **least vulnerable spot**

6. scarce
7. drunkard
8. noble
9. "Round up the usual suspects."
10. "I think this is the beginning of a beautiful friendship."
11. gin joint
12. human beings
13. carrying charges
14. hill of beans
15. I was misinformed
16. It is too far away to plan.
17. God Bless You
18. "Round up the usual suspects"
19. Ilsa
20. water his garden with it
21. Rick's
22. sentimentalist
23. "stick his neck out"
24. Rounding up twice the number of usual suspects
25. Here's looking at you, kid?
26. a "wow" finish
27. suspicious
28. a patriot
29. Mr. & Mrs. Victor Laszlo
30. "understand even less"

Factoid:

Many of the 34 nationalities that participated in the making of *Casablanca* were in fact refugees from Europe. This included major stars like Conrad Veidt, Peter Lorre, and Paul Henreid, as well as the numerous bit players who gave the film much of its authenticity.

"I beg of you, M'sieur, watch yourself. Be on guard. This place is full of vultures, vultures, everywhere, everywhere."

~ *the pickpocket* ~

Chapter 2
More Script & Lines

The American Film Institute's list of the "100 Most Famous Lines in Film History," includes seven lines from *Casablanca*, far more than any other film. The Epstein Brothers provided most of the humor and sarcasm, Howard Koch shaped the political slant, Casey Robinson the romance, and others like Hal Wallis and even Humphrey Bogart made contributions.

Questions:

1. After he first meets Victor Laszlo, what does Rick congratulate him for?

2. What crime does Renault charge Laszlo with when he arrests him?

3. What does Rick say in response to Laszlo being arrested by the *gendarmes*?

4. Renault's explanation for why Rick has seemingly betrayed Laszlo is that _____ has triumphed over _____ .

5. What does Laszlo say will happen to the world if we stop fighting our enemies?

6. What secret did Victor and Ilsa keep, even from their closest friends?

7. What is it that Laszlo seems to know all about, as it pertains to Rick, according to Rick?

8. When Rick asks Ilsa to shoot him, he says she will be doing him a _____ .

9. What is Rick referring to when he tells Laszlo, "What of it? "Then it will be out of its misery?"

10. In the opening scene, what does the narrator repeat a number of times that people do in Casablanca?

11. As he is talking to Laszlo, what expensive hobby does Rick say he had in the past, but will no longer have?

12. When Renault chides Rick for interfering in his little romances, Rick tells him to put it down as a gesture to what sentiment?

13. When Ilsa offers Rick a franc for his thoughts, he says in America that would only bring how much money?

14. When she comes to ask him for advice regarding Renault, what is the final advice that Rick gives to Annina (Bulgarian girl)?

15. As the Germans approach Paris, what does Rick call the German blacklist that he is on?

16. What two details did Rick remember regarding the Germans marching into Paris, that he mentions over drinks with Victor and Ilsa the first night in Casablanca?

17. Rick tells Strasser that his interest in whether Laszlo goes or stays in Casablanca is purely a _____ .

18. Complete this line: "Of all the gin joints in all the towns in all the world _____ ."

19. According to Renault, what gross understatement has he been informed about regarding Ilsa Lund?

20. What animal does Rick compare the Germans to, when he indicates he understands their point of view?

21. According to Renault, what is it about Rick that makes him a citizen of the world?

22. Because Renault romances almost all women, Rick says that when it comes to women Renault is a true _____ .

23. The romantic in Renault likes to think that the reason Rick came to Casablanca is because he _____ .

24. What is it that Renault tells Strasser he cannot regulate, even though he is trying to cooperate with the German government?

25. What lucky break did the two German couriers get by their deaths, according to Rick?

26. Rick says that the guy standing on the station platform in Paris had what type of look on his face, because his "insides had been kicked out?"

27. How does Rick toast Ilsa when she says "no questions," in response to his four questions about her past?

28. What does Rick say he did in his apartment in Paris so that the Germans would know where to find him?

29. When Rick says, "Maybe not today, maybe not tomorrow, but soon, and for the rest of your life" what is he referring to?

30. What is Rick's reply to Annina's question, "If someone loved you very much, so that your happiness was the only thing that she wanted in the whole world, but she did a bad thing to make certain of it, could you forgive her?"

Answers:

1. **his work**
2. **accessory to murder**
3. **destiny has taken a hand**
4. **love, virtue**
5. **it will die**
6. **their marriage**
7. **his destiny**
8. **favor**
9. **the death of the world**
10. **wait, and wait, and wait, and wait**
11. **fighting on the side of the underdog**
12. **love**

13. penny
14. go back to Bulgaria
15. their role of honor
16. the Germans wore gray, Ilsa wore blue
17. sporting one
18. she walks into "mine"
19. she is the most beautiful woman to ever visit Casablanca
20. hound
21. he is a drunkard
22. democrat
23. killed a man
24. the feelings of the people
25. they became the honored dead
26. comical
27. "Here's looking at you, kid"
28. left a note in his apartment
29. Ilsa will regret it if she does not go with Victor
30. "Nobody ever loved me that much."

Factoid:

Bogart changed the original script line, "Here's good luck to you, kid," to his signature line, "Here's looking at you, kid." His signature line never appears in the script.

Factoid:

French, German, American English, British English, and Russian are all languages spoken in *Casablanca*.

"Moonlight and love songs never out of date;
Hearts full of passion, jealousy and hate;
Women needs man and man must have his mate:"

~ *"As Time Goes By"* ~

Chapter 3
Music, Songs & Lyrics

Another outstanding feature of *Casablanca* is the musical score put together by Max Steiner. Combining many old standards with new material he wrote and arranged, the music and lyrics greatly enhance the enjoyment of the film. "As Time Goes By" has been consistently voted the greatest movie song of all time, although it was not written specifically for *Casablanca*.

Questions:

1. The signature song of *Casablanca* was what tune that had actually been a minor hit eleven years earlier?

2. Which major creative force in *Casablanca* hated "As Time Goes By" and wanted to replace it with his own song?

3. "What do two lovers do when they say I love you?"

4. Which two things are never out of date according to "As Time Goes By?"

5. Rick actually says to Sam, "You played it for her and you can play it for me. If she can stand it, I can! Play it!" instead of which often misquoted line?

6. What had Ingrid Bergman done to herself for her role in *For Whom The Bell Tolls,* which made it impossible to re-shoot scenes that would have replaced the song "As Time Goes By?"

7. The colotura soprano, nightclub performer, who sang "Tango des Roses" as she plays it on her guitar, is which singer?

8. What song from *Casablanca* is on the Hit Parade radio show for 21 straight weeks in 1943?

9. Instead of "As Time Goes By," what original song written specifically for *Casablanca*, was expected to be the big hit?

10. Which actor/musician, who had tested for the role of Sam, actually played the songs on the piano in the film while Dooley Wilson copied his movements?

11. What lyric follows "my hair is curley" in "Knock on Wood?"

12. Victor Laszlo shows his leadership qualities when he leads the night-club audience in the singing of the _____ .

13. What song is playing when the German officers come into Rick's Café the second night in Casablanca?

14. What song is playing at the beginning of the opening scene in Rick's Café?

15. What does Rick do, while Sam sings, "Knock on Wood?"

16. What song is playing when Ilsa and Rick are dancing the rumba in the Paris nightclub?

17. "The same old story" is a fight between what two sentiments according to "As Time Goes By?"

18. The song that the German officers attempt to sing in Rick's Café, that is drowned out by the French national anthem is _____ .

19. "As Time Goes By," written by Herman Hupfeld for the 1931 musical, "Everyone's Welcome," became a hit song for what performer known for singing through his nose and using a megaphone to amplify his "thin" voice?

20. What song is being played when Rick first appears on the screen in the film?

21. According to "As Time Goes By" hearts are full of passion and what two other things?

22. What song is playing when Sacha kisses Rick, after he has helped Jan win at roulette?

23. "You Must Have Been a Beautiful Baby" is playing when which character walks into Rick's with a German officer?

24. The man who wrote "As Time Goes By" in 1933 is _____ .

25. What song is being played when Renault informs Rick that an arrest is going to be made in his café?

26. Besides the drums, what four instruments are played by the band at Rick's Café?

27. When Rick tells Ilsa about a story he has heard many times, it goes along with what instrument that is playing in the parlor downstairs?

28. What song that the nightclub singer Corinna Murra sings, had its rights purchased for a one-time fee of $180?

29. What song is Sam playing when Ferrari offers him a job at the Blue Parrot?

30. When Ilsa enters Rick's Café for the first time the band is playing what song?

Answers:

1. **"As Time Goes Bye"**
2. **Max Steiner**
3. **woo**
4. **moonlight & love songs**
5. **play it again Sam**
6. **cut her hair**
7. **Corina Murra**
8. **"As Time Goes By"**
9. **"Knock on Wood"**
10. **Elliot Carpentar**
11. **my teeth are pearly**

12. *"Marseilles"*
13. "If I Could be with You"
14. "It Had to be You"
15. hides the "Letters of Transit" in the piano
16. "Perfidia"
17. love and glory
18. "Watch on the Rhine"
19. Rudy Vallee
20. "Crazy Rhythm"
21. jealousy and hate
22. "The Very Thought of You"
23. Yvonne
24. Herman Hupfeld
25. "Baby Face"
26. trombone, accordion, trumpet, clarinet
27. tinny piano
28. "Tango des Roses"
29. "A Blossom Fell"
30. "Speak to Me of Love"

Factoid:

Along with the Academy Award for Best Picture, *Casablanca* won Oscars for Best Director, Michael Curtiz, and Best Screenplay with Julius & Philip Epstein and Howard Koch sharing the honors, along with other writers like Casey Robinson who also made a contribution. Arthur Edeson for cinematography, Owen Marks for film editing, and Max Steiner for music score were all nominated, but failed to win.

"But not everybody could get to Lisbon directly; and so, a tortuous, roundabout refugee trail sprang up. Paris to Marseilles, across the Mediterranean to Oran, then by train, or auto, or foot, across the rim of Africa to Casablanca in French Morocco."

~ Narrator ~

Chapter 4
Geography

Although not a road or travel film, there are many references to geographic places in Europe, Africa, and North America sprinkled throughout *Casablanca*. These geographic references help to illuminate the story and give the film its international quality.

Questions:

1. What is the name of the city in North Africa where most of the action in the film takes place?

2. The capital of France where the flashback scene occurs, and Rick and Ilsa have their romance before the Germans arrive, is what city?

3. The region of the world in the western hemisphere where freedom still existed, and it became the ultimate destination for most of the refugees is what country?

4. What is the name of the town in northern France where Victor Laszlo refused to leave Ilsa after she became ill?

5. The city in southern France where Rick and Ilsa were headed as the Germans entered Paris, is what Mediterranean port city?

6. A port city in Algeria where refugees arrived after escaping from the Nazis in Europe, is what city?

7. What country in East Africa did Rick run guns to in 1935, as it fought against the Italian Fascists invasion?

8. What country in Europe is where Rick had fought on the Loyalist side against the Fascists in 1936?

9. When Rick refuses to let the German banker gamble at his *Café Amercain*, what city, that was a possession of the United States, did the German mention as a place where he had gambled?

10. What city in the United States, where Rick was born, does he advise Strasser and the Nazis not to invade certain sections of it?

11. What is the eastern European country where Jan and Annina are from, "where the devil has the people by the throat" according to Annina?

12. The capital city of unoccupied France, after the Germans occupied France in WWII, is what city that is also the government of French West Africa?

13. The homeland of Victor Laszlo, that is taken over by the Germans is what country?

14. When Ilsa asks Sam to play some of the old songs, the first one he plays is the name of what city located on Catalina Island in the United States?

15. The homeland for both Berger (member of the underground) and Ilsa Lund is what Scandinavian country?

16. The city where Heinze asks Rick if he can imagine the Germans in that city, and Rick responds, "Ask me when you get there," is what city?

17. The home city of Victor Laszlo where he published anti-Nazi newspaper articles in his cellar until he was captured is _____ .

18. When Strasser tries to disparage the Americans by calling them "blundering," Renault mentions what city as one that they "blundered" into in 1918?

19. The great embarkation point where Europeans could leave for America is what city?

20. The man gambling in Rick's Café, who, in an attempt to impress Carl, claimed he had run the second largest banking house in what European city?

21. The desert where Casablanca is located and where Strasser says the Germans must get used to all climates, is what desert?

22. The country in eastern Europe, with the opposite type of climate from Casablanca that the Germans have to get used to, is what country?

23. A city in French Equatorial Africa where a Free-French garrison is located, and where Rick and Louis decide to go to fight against the Germans, is what city?

24. The capital of Norway, where Ilsa had lived before she went to Paris, is what city?

25. The city that is a stopover point for the plane from Casablanca to Lisbon, is what Moroccan city?

26. The 1990 Sydney Pollack-Robert Redford movie that reused many of the elements from *Casablanca*, is named for what city in North America?

27. The two German couriers were murdered on the train that was coming from what city in North Africa?

28. What two cities do refugees have to travel through in Morocco, before they get to Casablanca?

29. The name change from the stage play to the film was inspired by what popular 1938 exotic melodrama, that was also named for a North African city?

30. Strasser mentions that there are Resistance Groups in what eight European cities?

Answers:

1. **Casablanca**
2. **Paris**
3. **Americas**

4. Lille
5. Marseilles
6. Oran
7. Ethiopia
8. Spain
9. Honolulu
10. New York
11. Bulgaria
12. Vichy
13. Czechoslovakia
14. Avalon
15. Norway
16. London
17. Prague
18. Berlin
19. Lisbon
20. Amsterdam
21. Sahara
22. Russia
23. Brazzaville
24. Oslo
25. Tangier
26. Havana
27. Oran
28. Fez and Meknes
29. *Algiers*
30. Oslo, Brussels, Paris, Amsterdam, Berlin, Prague, Belgrade, Athens

Factoid:

After he came to America, Conrad Veidt who played Major Strasser, donated most of his salary from his films to British War Relief. He had become a British citizen after leaving Germany.

"Vive La France! Vive la democracie"
"Vive La France! Vive la democracie"

~ Yvonne and crowd ~

Chapter 5
Foreign Words & Terms

To be absolutely authentic *Casablanca* could have been filmed in French with English subtitles. This may have hurt the box office. As it is, there are just enough foreign phrases (usually French) spaced throughout the film to give it an international flair.

Foreign terms and phrases are varied and are in the following languages: French, German, Russian, Italian, and British English.

Questions:

1. The toast given by the Englishman at the bar is what common British expression?

2. What is the name of the French police officers who would often "round up the usual suspects" in the film?

3. What is the name of Hitler's government that means third empire?

4. What French city known for its mineral water, became the capital of France after France was occupied by the Germans?

5. What does the four word French sign that is on the side of the building at the airport say?

6. The term for "good-bye" in French used by Ilsa and others in *Casablanca*, is what expression?

7. What is the term for "mister" in French, used by Victor Laszlo when addressing Rick as well as by others in the film?

8. When Yvonne comes into Rick's with a German officer, the French officer at the bar mutters what derogatory term to describe the German?

9. What is the Italian address for "mister" that is used as a title for the owner of the Blue Parrot, Ferrari?

10. Petain's picture is next to the words, "Je tiens mes promesses meme celles des autres," that mean?

11. The Leuchtags use what German term of endearment that means "my dear," to address each other?

12. When the German of the *Deutchesbank* is refused entry to Rick's Casino, he threatens to report this to what Nazi propaganda newspaper, whose name means "attack?"

13. What is the French term for "miss" or "missus," used to describe Ilsa by both Louis Renault and Strasser?

14. What type of liqueur does Victor Laszlo order for himself and Ilsa that has a distinctly French name?

15. What is the German term for "mister," used to describe Heinze and also used by Strasser in addressing Laszlo?

16. The name of the French train station heading south to Marseilles, where Rick and Sam are "stood up" by Ilsa?

17. *Veuve Cliquot 26* is the name of what French product that Renault recommends to Strasser?

18. What is the name of the secret police of the Nazi political party?

19. What type of French money is used in the film with an exchange rate of 44 to 1 to the U.S. dollar?

20. What is the toast by Sacha that is the Russian equivalent of "cheers?"

21. *"Wacht am Rhein"* is a patriotic song sung by Strasser and the other German officers, and its title means _____ .

22. What is the title of chief of police held by Louis Renault, that described his position as the administrator in charge of a geographic department, who functioned under the control of the central government as both a civil magistrate and a policeman?

23. What is the inscription on the *Palais de Justice* carved in a marble block along the roofline of the building?

24. After Strasser receives the phone call from Renault, he orders the officer to get his car quickly, and the officer responds by saying what German expression meaning "as you ordered?"

25. What is the name of the French national anthem that when sung under the leadership of Victor Laszlo, leads to Rick's Café being closed down by Louis Renault?

26. The name of Rick's is *Café Americain* which means _____ .

27. At the conclusion of the singing of the "Marseilles," what does Yvonne shout out that the crowd repeats, that means "hurrah for France?"

28. What is the type of mineral water or sparkling water that is named for the French town that became the capital of unoccupied France?

29. When Mr. Leuchtag asks Mrs. Leuchtag "what watch?" he is asking her for the _____ .

30. Yvonne leads the crowd shouting out what French expression after the singing of the "Marseilles," that means "hurrah for democracy?"

Answers:

1. **cheerio**
2. *gendarmes*
3. **Third Reich**
4. **Vichy**
5. *"Defense Absolue de Fumer"*
6. *au revoir*

7. Monsieur
8. *boche*
9. *Signor*
10. I keep my promises, just as I keep the promises of others.
11. *liebchen*
12. *Angriff*
13. *Mademoiselle*
14. *cointreaux*
15. *Herr*
16. *Gare de Lyon*
17. wine
18. *Gestapo*
19. franc
20. *nostrovia*
21. watch on the Rhine
22. *Prefect*
23. *Liberte, Egalite, Fraternite*
24. *Zu Befehl*
25. *Marseilles*
26. American Café
27. *Viva La France*
28. *Vichy*
29. time
30. *Viva La Democracie*

Factoid:

The *Angriff*, that the member of the *Deutchesbank* is going to report Rick to, is a German newspaper started by Joseph Goebbels in 1927 that preached the Nazi line and denounced Jews, Communists, and anyone else the Germans did not like.

"Henri wants us to finish this bottle and then three more. He says he'll water his garden with champagne before he'll let the Germans drink any of it."

~ Richard Blaine ~

Chapter 6
The Many Drinks
in Casablanca

The drinking of beverages – especially alcoholic ones – plays a significant role in *Casablanca*. Much of the conversation and action revolves around the drinking of a great variety of cocktails.

Many of these answers are generic – cocktail, wine, coffee, champagne etc. – but some are very specific. Depending upon the information in the film, give either a generic or specific answer.

Questions:

1. What are the English couple drinking, as they are approached by the pickpocket, in the opening scene at the outside café (generic)?

2. What type of drink does Ferrari offer Rick in the Blue Parrot when Rick asks for his shipment from the bus? Rick refuses the drink and says he never drinks in the morning (specific).

3. What is the man who is buying passage on the fishing "smack" (ketch) *Santiago* drinking, as he negotiates the deal (generic)?

4. What is Signor Ferrari drinking as he sits down at a table the first night in Rick's Café (specific)?

5. What kind of drink glass is empty and sitting in front of Rick as he is playing chess (generic)?

6. As he toasts Sacha with "cheerio," what type of drink is the Englishmen drinking at the bar (generic)?

7. What type of alcohol is Rick getting drunk on late the first night at his café when Ilsa walks in on him (specific)?

8. What drink does Victor Laszlo order as he joins Berger at the bar (specific)?

9. What is the woman drinking who is trying to get more money for her jewels when selling them to the Moor (generic)?

10. What type of drink is on the top of Sam's piano while he sings "Knock on Wood" (specific)?

11. What type of glass does Rick set upright, after the disturbance that occurs when Ugarte is arrested?

12. What are Ilsa and Rick drinking in Rick's room, the second night in Casablanca (specific)?

13. What type of drink does Victor Laszlo order for himself and Ilsa, as they sit down the first night at Rick's Café (specific)?

14. What type of drink does Carl serve to the Leuchtags (older German couple), when he joins them to celebrate their going to America?

15. What type of drink is Renault given in Rick's office (specific)?

16. Ugarte is drinking what type of drink while talking to Rick (generic)?

17. What is the type of drink Louis Renault is drinking at the outside table at Rick's (specific)?

18. After Rick has helped Jan and Annina what type of drink (generic) does Carl offer to get Rick, but Rick refuses?

19. What type of drink does Renault order for himself and Laszlo, while they are sitting at the bar as Berger leaves (specific)?

20. What type of liquor is Sacha serving Yvonne that he calls Boss' private stock (specific)?

21. Rick refers to his bar as what type of place, named after a specific type of liquor (specific)?

22. "A bottle of their best" is what type of liquor that Renault orders, when he is invited by Laszlo to join him and Ilsa at their table (specific)?

23. As they are sitting at an outside table in Paris at the *Café Pierre*, what two different types of drinks are Rick and Ilsa drinking (specific & generic)?

24. What is Rick drinking at the bar, and Carl tries to take it away from him, after Rick has helped Jan and Annina (specific)?

25. What type of drink does Ilsa thank Ferrari for at the Blue Parrot? She says she will miss it when they leave Casablanca (specific).

26. What type of drink does Rick give Laszlo, to help him get over the injury he suffered in escaping from the break-up of the Resistance meeting (specific)?

27. What type of cocktail does Yvonne order when she comes in with the German officer (specific)?

28. What are Rick, Ilsa, and Sam drinking at Henri's *La Belle Aurora* as the Germans are beginning to occupy Paris (specific)?

29. Renault starts to pour himself a drink of _____ after Rick has shot Strasser; but in a symbolic act drops the bottle and the glass into the trash can (specific).

30. Instead of champagne, what is the name of the French wine that Renault recommends to Strasser, to accompany the order of a tin of caviar?

Answers:

1. **wine**
2. **cocktail**
3. **wine**

4. **Turkish Coffee**
5. **champagne**
6. **cocktail (tall)**
7. **bourbon**
8. **Champagne Cocktail**
9. **wine**
10. **water glass**
11. **wine**
12. **champagne**
13. **cointreaux**
14. **brandy**
15. **brandy**
16. **wine**
17. **cognac or brandy**
18. **coffee**
19. **Champagne Cocktail**
20. **brandy**
21. **gin**
22. **champagne**
23. **coffee and wine**
24. **brandy**
25. **Turkish Coffee**
26. **whiskey**
27. **French 77's**
28. **champagne**
29. **Vichy water**
30. **Veuve Cliquot '26**

Factoid:

When she hosted "Saturday Night Live," Candace Bergman played Ilsa to John Belushi's Rick in one of the most memorable parodies of *Casablanca*.

"I'm sorry, Madame, but diamonds are a drug on the market.
Everybody sells diamonds. There are diamonds everywhere."

~ *Moor* ~

Chapter 7
Scenes, Images & Visuals

Modern viewers sometimes fail to see the genuine artistry that can accompany a black and white film. The visual imagery and props in *Casablanca* are some of the films most memorable features. Who does not remember the shadows on the walls, the shading of Ingrid Bergman's face, and the effective use of props such as ceiling fans?

Questions:

1. What animal is in a cage outside of Ferrari's establishment?

2. What does Carl bring to the table of the older German couple who are going to America?

3. What color is the square that Jan Brandel bets on with Rick's advice?

4. What is the weather like when Rick and Sam are at the *Gare de Lyon* train station in Paris?

5. What does Ilsa do as Rick is kissing her for the last time in Paris?

6. In the opening scene what did the Englishman first think that he had left in his hotel?

7. What is uncharacteristic about the weather in Casablanca when Victor and Ilsa get on the plane to Lisbon?

8. When Rick offers Louis a drink of brandy in his office, he pours it from what type of container?

9. What instrument does the nightclub singer at Rick's Café play?

10. What is Rick writing on the check in the opening scene in Rick's Café?

11. What are the weather conditions when Strasser arrives?

12. Who is the only major character who never smokes in the film?

13. What symbol is on the tail fin of the plane that arrives in Casablanca in the opening scene?

14. When Rick and Ilsa are dancing in the Paris nightclub, what 1970s piece of decorative regalia is prominent in the scene?

15. Which chess piece does Rick immediately touch after writing "OK, Rick" on the check in the opening scene in his café?

16. What symbol is on the side of the German tank in the newsreel footage?

17. Which chess piece is Rick getting ready to move as he talks with Ugarte?

18. What do the characters do 22 times in the film that would not be considered acceptable today?

19. What item in the film did the Japanese Trading Firm of C. Itoh & Co. purchase for $154,000 in 1988?

20. What was it that Rick took into Ethiopia in 1935 that showed he was on the side of the underdog?

21. Because Rick is in such a hurry to sell his club to Ferrari, the deal is sealed by a _____ .

22. According to the Moor who is buying gems, what is it that is everywhere in Casablanca and a drug on the market?

23. What are they drinking when Rick first toasts Ilsa with "Here's looking at you, kid?"

24. What type of flower does Rick wear in his lapel in the final flashback scene with Ilsa in Paris?

25. What is the new "German 77" that Rick refers to in the film?

26. The type of Latin dance that Rick and Ilsa are dancing in the nightclub is the _____ .

27. What object is on each table at Rick's Café?

28. What gesture does Sam make after Rick asks him to play "As Time Goes By" the second night in Rick's Café?

29. What was the cause of Victor Laszlo's injury when he escaped from the Resistance meeting that was raided by the police?

30. What was unique about the extras who were hired to be the mechanics at the airport?

Answers:
1. parrot
2. brandy
3. black
4. raining
5. knocks over a glass
6. his wallet
7. foggy
8. decanter
9. guitar
10. OK, Rick
11. clear & sunny (hot)
12 Ilsa Lund
13 Swastika
14. disco ball
15. white bishop
16. Iron Cross
17. black king
18. smoke cigarettes
19. Sam's piano
20. guns
21. handshake
22. diamonds
23. champagne
24. daisy

25. **cannon or gun**
26. **rumba**
27. **lamps**
28. **shakes his head**
29. **broken window**
30. **vertically challenged (midgets or little people)**

Factoid:

The chess game in the film was an actual game that Bogart was playing with Irving Kovner of Brooklyn.

Factoid:

Boris III, the absolute ruler of Bulgaria and a supporter of Nazi Germany, is "the devil" that the newly married Annina is referring to.

Factoid:

Because of the war and the blackouts in Los Angeles, summer shooting days for *Casablanca* ended by 6:30 PM so that everyone could get home before dark.

Factoid:

From the original play, the names of Martinez and Rinaldo were changed to Ferrari and Renault, because there was great sensitivity to the Latin American market and the names were too "Spanish" sounding. Both Ferrari and Renault were names of Italian and French automobiles that were well known in the United States.

"I was informed you were the most beautiful woman ever to visit Casablanca. That was a gross understatement."

~ Louis Renault ~

Chapter 8
More Scenes, Images & Visuals

Some of the more difficult questions regarding scenes, images, and visuals, can only be answered by discerning viewers. It takes great visual acumen to deal with many of these questions as well as a quick hand with the pause button on the DVD.

Questions:

1. What are Rick and Ilsa eating as they ride on the boat during the Paris flashback scene?

2. What does Rick keep in the inside pocket on the right side of his jacket?

3. What adornment is attached to Mrs. Leuchtag's hat?

4. What is the emblem on the side of the fuselage of the plane that Victor and Ilsa take when they leave Casablanca for Lisbon?

5. What is Rick doing when he first appears on the screen?

6. What kind of flag is behind Rick and Ilsa when they are on the boat on the *Seine* in Paris?

7. What garment of attire does Ilsa wear the second night in Rick's, that Ferrari wore the first night?

8. The three medals that Renault wears on his uniform are

   _____ .

9. When he meets Victor and Ilsa at his café, what type of head covering is Ferrari wearing?

10. What article of clothing does Strasser put on after Victor and Ilsa leave Renault's office?

11. When the German from the *Deutchesbank* is refused entry into Rick's Casino, what does he hand to Rick that Rick tears up?

12. What is the basic design of the tablecloths and the curtains in *La Belle Aurora*?

13. What is Ilsa doing when she and Rick are shown in the Paris apartment for the first time?

14. What symbol of the Resistance is on the ring that Berger shows to Victor Laszlo?

15. Which black chess piece is Rick fiddling with during his conversation with Ugarte?

16. When Louis Renault is sitting at a table and talking to Rick in front of the café, what three items are on the table in front of him?

17. Along with their double-breasted white tuxedos, what accessory item do Rick, Sam, and Ugarte also wear?

18. What chess piece has Rick captured in the chess match?

19. What are the first three letters on the side of the plane that is going to Lisbon?

20. What do Ferrari and Rick have to drink when they are settling the deal of the sale of Rick's Café?

21. What two words are on the "papers" of the man who is shot in the opening scene?

22. What decoration/adornment that is typically Moroccan in style, is on the lamp shades, awnings, umbrellas, and drapes?

23. What is superimposed on the screen as the narrator describes the refugee trail that goes across the Mediterranean from Europe to Africa?

24. Who is the last person seen on the screen in the Paris flashback sequence?

25. What words are on the paddy wagon as it rounds up the refugees in the opening scene?

26. What type of plane is seen taking off at the end of the film?

27. The sign on Rick's Café said it had been closed by order of the _____ .

28. What is the specific location at the Prefect of Police building where Rick will make the arrangements for Laszlo to pick up the "Letters of Transit?"

29. What is the last thing that Rick does when he gets on the train to Marseilles with Sam?

30. After Louis Renault drops the bottle of Vichy water into the trash can at the airport, what does he do that signifies he is no longer a part of the French collaboration government?

Answers:

1. **nuts (probably peanuts)**
2. **cigarette case**
3. **flowers**
4. **Pegasus**
5. **signing a check**
6. **French tricolor**
7. **cummerbund**
8. **French Legion of Honor, WWI French Victory Medal, & WWI French Commemorative Medal**
9. **fez**
10. **gloves**
11. **a business card**
12. **checks**
13. **arranging flowers**

14. **Cross of Lorraine**
15. **king**
16. **a glass, a bottle, & an ash tray**
17. **bow tie**
18. **white bishop**
19. **FAM**
20. **Turkish Coffee**
21. **"Free French"**
22. **fringe**
23. **ships**
24. **train conductor**
25. **Ville de Casablanca**
26. **Lockheed Electra 12A**
27. *Prefect of Police*
28. **visitors pen**
29. **throws away Ilsa's note**
30. **kicks the trash can**

Factoid:

While *Casablanca* was filming, Marcel Dalio, the croupier, filed for divorce from his wife Madeleine LeBeau (Yvonne) on the grounds of desertion.

Factoid:

Initially, preview audiences were not impressed with *Casablanca* until "destiny took a hand." In November of 1942, a few weeks after the preview, Anglo-American troops invaded North Africa. This invasion made the film topical which helped to launch its popularity.

"I remember every detail. The Germans wore gray, you wore blue."
~ Richard Blaine ~

Chapter 9
Clothing & Apparel

Casablanca had the unique distinction of being the first film restricted by WWII rationing. This had a great deal to do with both the look of the clothing as well as the materials that were used. Despite these restrictions, the signature look of *Casablanca* is fondly remembered and often emulated today.

Questions:

1. What does Rick always wear in his nightclub?

2. What is Ilsa wearing on her head when she visits Rick late the first night in his cafe?

3. What specific type of head covering is Ferrari wearing the first night when he comes to Rick's Café?

4. What does the English woman have in her hand in the opening scene with the pickpocket?

5. Besides Rick, who else also always wears a white tuxedo at Rick's Café?

6. What hand and which finger is Ilsa wearing a ring on?

7. What type of hat does the pickpocket wear when he bumps into Carl the second night at Rick's Café?

8. What adornment is attached to Mrs. Leuchtag's hat?

9. What distinctive and prominent design is on the Englishmen's tie in the opening scene?

10. What piece of jewelry does Ilsa wear to the café the first night that resembles a bird or a palm tree?

11. What symbol is on the outside left pocket of Strasser's uniform jacket?

12. Which type or style of purse does Ilsa carry?

13. What type of flower does Rick wear in his lapel in the opening scene in the Paris flashback?

14. Besides her hat, what other accessory item does Ilsa wear when she and Victor go to Renault's office?

15. Because of wartime rationing, all of Ingrid Bergman's clothing was made from what kind of fabric?

16. In the closing airport scene, which article of clothing did Bogart wear that became associated with his "persona?"

17. Rick's doorman, Abdul, wears what type of head covering?

18. What is Ilsa wearing when she is in her room with Rick in the flashback scene, when she offers him a franc for his thoughts?

19. What type of head covering is Ilsa wearing when she and Rick read about the Germans coming to Paris?

20. What is the pickpocket carrying when he talks with the English couple in the opening scene?

21. What hand and which finger does Rick wear a ring on?

22. What is the pattern on Yvonne's dress when she comes into Rick's Café with the German the second night?

23. Which major male character never wears either a tuxedo or a uniform?

24. The lace seller in the *medina* has what type of head covering?

25. What two characters carry walking sticks in the film?

26. In the opening scene, what is the Englishman wearing that would be considered an "affectation" today?

27. What type of hat is Rick wearing at the airport?

28. What different way does Rick wear his trench coat at the airport that becomes his signature look, and starts a fashion trend for men wearing that garment?

29. Ingrid Bergman's hair styling procedure is unique in that she did not allow her stylist to set her hair or use what common items in her hair?

30. Because of wartime rationing, clothing could not include what six items that were common accessories?

Answers:

1. **tuxedo**
2. **a scarf**
3. **Panama hat**
4. **a fan**
5. **Sam & Ugarte**
6. **pinky finger of the right hand**
7. **pith helmut**
8. **flowers**
9. **zebra stripes**
10. **broach**
11. **Iron Cross**
12. **clutch**
13. **carnation**
14. **gloves**
15. **cotton**
16. **trench coat**
17. **fez**
18. **a robe**
19. **beret**
20. **walking stick**
21. **3rd finger right hand**
22. **vertical stripes**
23. **Victor Laszlo**
24. **turban**

25. **pickpocket and Signor Ferrari**
26. **monocle**
27. **fedora (aka – snap brim)**
28. **tying not buckling the belt on his trench coat**
29. **hair pins or bobby pins**
30. **pleats, lace, patch pockets, cloth covered buttons, cuffs, & lapels for woolen suits**

Factoid:

Casablanca is one of the last film companies to use the Metropolitan Airport in Van Nuys (Strasser arrival scene); the airport was taken over by the Army Air Corps for use as a military base during the war.

Factoid:

Ingrid Bergman's costumes, which would have normally been made of silk or wool, were made of cotton because of war time restrictions and rationing.

Factoid:

According to War Limitation Orders M73 and L75, the motion picture industry had to eliminate, pleats, patch pockets, cloth covered buttons, cuffs on pants, and lapels for woolen suit's from its films. *Casablanca* became the first all cotton film.

"They grab Ugarte and she walks in. Well, that's the way it goes. One in, one out."

~ Richard Blaine ~

Chapter 10
Flaws, Mistakes & Goofs

Despite the fact that the script was being written while the film was shooting, *Casablanca* has few goofs, mistakes, or flaws – but there are some. There are a number of things that could have been done to make the film more plausible; however, some of the "hokum" – especially regarding the "Letters in Transit" – give the film much of its charm.

Questions:

1. It is pouring rain and Rick and Sam are about to leave Paris for Marseilles. In the shot where Rick is actually on the train as it pulls away from the station, what is now dry?

2. Rick lights a new cigarette just as he is about to sit down and talk to Renault outside the club the first night. As Tonelli and Caselle come by arguing as usual, Rick is seen _____ .

3. When Strasser arrives at the airport and gets out of the car, there are no epaulets on his coat; however, when he walks toward the phone _____ .

4. As Strasser turns to talk to Rick on his way to the phone, there are no epaulets on his coat; but as he picks up the phone and shoots at Rick _____ .

5. As the member of the Free French Resistance is shot in the opening scene, there is nothing in front of the picture of Petain and his slogan on the wall. But as the *gendarmes* search the man and find the "Cross of Lorraine" papers, what three items are now in front of, and to the left of, the Petain poster?

6. When Strasser tells Renault that Rick is just another "blundering" American, Renault reminds him that he was with the Americans when they "blundered" into Berlin in 1918. Although they were part of the "occupation," the Americans never _____ .

7. What unlikely feature does the car have when Rick and Ilsa are driving in Paris?

8. The day the Germans marched into Paris, Ilsa is wearing a pinstriped suit and white blouse instead of a _____ .

9. When Rick is getting drunk after hours in his café, he laments that they are asleep all over America, and asleep in New York. What time would it actually be in America?

10. When Ugarte sits down to talk with Rick he is carrying a black Homberg style hat; but when he goes to cash his chips with the *gendarmes* _____ .

11. Jan is down to 6 chips when Rick tells him to bet on 22. Assuming these are 1 franc chips, and he wins twice by letting it ride, rather than the couple of thousand that Emil says he won, the amount he would have won would be _____ .

12. The so-called "Letters of Transit" signed by DeGaulle would have no value in *Casablanca* because _____ .

13. In order for the "Letters of Transit" to be valid, who's signature would have to be on them (Supreme Military Commander of French North Africa)?

14. Actually, even Weygand might not be correct as a signature on the "Letters of Transit," because he had been removed from his command 11 days before the "Letters" were stolen, and he had been replaced by _____ .

15. While in their hotel room, Victor tells Ilsa "our faithful friend" is still there as they see the man who is following them hiding behind a building. When Victor leaves for the Resistance meeting he walks _____ .

16. What climactic condition (it almost never occurs in Casablanca) is used in the final scene to disguise the "cheesy" nature of the miniature cut-out plane on the runway?

17. Major Strasser is portrayed as an urbane, sophisticated man; yet, the first two times he eats caviar, he eats it in an uncouth manner directly from a _____ .

18. After picking up the white knight in the chess game, Rick is interrupted by the disturbance with the German banker. After going to the door, he sits down with Ugarte and the white knight is mysteriously _____ .

19. For the most part, *Casablanca* had good intentions regarding racial stereotyping, but there is one major slip-up. What term does Ilsa call Sam, that would be inappropriate for a 26 year old woman to call a 54 year old man?

20. When Strasser sits down and orders caviar the first night, the Reservee sign is clearly on the table as the waiter leaves. The next shot of the table when Ugarte is being arrested shows _____ .

21. In the closing scene, Rick and Louis walk across the runway in the opposite direction from the automobiles, presumably on their way to Brazzaville. They are walking in the _____ .

22. The wine glass that gets knocked over after the arrest of Ugarte becomes a _____ .

23. In the credits, the Hungarian actor S.Z. Sakall, who plays Carl, is called _____ .

24. While he is listening to Annina's story, after Rick sets his glass down, the next shot shows it has turned into a _____ .

25. After the café has been closed Rick is talking to Carl, who is wearing his glasses on his forehead. In the next shot Carl's glasses are _____ .

26. Renault talks about two precedents being broken when Victor and Ilsa come in to Rick's Café. This is incorrect because precedents are not broken, they are _____ .

27. In the café scene at *La Belle Aurora,* Bogart sets his drink next to Ilsa's glass. But when they kiss, she knocks over one glass and the other glass is _____ .

28. When Ilsa is in their hotel room, she is shown from behind looking out the window at the street below through a roll-type window shade; and when she is shown again the window shade is _____ .

29. When Rick goes to see Ferrari at the Blue Parrot the first time, there is a bottle on the table between them. Ferrari is shown taking the cap off the bottle, pouring a drink, and then returning the cap to the bottle. In the next two cuts the bottle is

_____ .

30. When Rick is talking about the German guns shelling near Paris, he describes them as "77's." This is an error as no "77's" existed and the guns were probably _____ .

Answer:

1. **his raincoat**
2. **lighting another cigarette**
3. **the epaulets appear**
4. **the epaulets have returned**
5. **a chair, a doll, and a vessel or vase**
6. **were in Berlin**
7. **steering wheel on the British side not the continental side**
8. **blue dress**
9. **assuming it is around 11:00 or midnight after his bar closed, it would be late afternoon on the west coast and early evening in New York – they would hardly be asleep in "the city that never sleeps."**

10. the hat is missing
11. 7,776 francs
12. it was governed by Vichy not the Free French
13. General Weygand
14. General Alphonse Juin
15. walks right by the spot where the man had been hiding
16. fog
17. spoon
18. on the chess board and has been moved from its original position
19. boy
20. the sign removed
21. in the wrong direction
22. whiskey glass
23. S.K. Sakall
24. cigarette
25. on his nose
26. set
27. not on the table
28. slat-type Venetian blinds
29. gone, and in the cut after that the bottle is back, but without the cap
30. 88's

Factoid:

An obvious "goof" or mistake in the film occurs as Rick is getting soaked in the rain at the Paris train station, but when he actually boards the train his raincoat is dry.

Factoid:

Although the Office of War Information liked the references to the underground resistance to the Nazis, it was unhappy with the negative portrayal of Vichy France, especially the role of Louis Renault.

Factoid:

No one ever says "Play it Again Sam" in the film. The closest to this line is when Humphrey Bogart says to Sam, "You played it for her you can play it for me … If she can stand it, I can. Play it!"

Factoid:

Bogart's signature line, "Here's looking at you, kid!" was originally in the script as "Here's good luck to you, kid," until he changed it. His new line never appears in the script.

Factoid:

The Office of War Information, government officials in charge of propaganda that acted as a censoring board, set up its Bureau of Motion Pictures office three weeks after *Casablanca's* script was first written, which made the script relatively free of censorship.

Factoid:

From 1990 to 1991 in the *New Republic, Newsday, The Washington Post, Daily Variety, Los Angeles Times*, and *The New York Times* there are nearly 100 references to Renault's line that has become a metaphor for hypocrisy, "I'm shocked! Shocked to find that gambling is going on here!"

Factoid:

The German officers originally sang "Horst Wessel," but that song had to be replaced by "Watch on the Rhine" because it was under German copyright protection.

"Are you one of those people who cannot imagine the Germans in their beloved Paris?"

~ Major Heinrich Strasser ~

Chapter 11
Actors' Backgrounds

With such a rich and varied cast, the background of the actors in *Casablanca* provides a study in human diversity. In fact, only three of the 14 actors appearing in the credits were born in the United States. This multinational cast, many of them actual refugees from Europe, brought to the set a sense of verisimilitude, as many of them had actually experienced what characters in *Casablanca* were experiencing.

Questions:

1. What actor, who's real name is Arthur, got his nickname by playing Irish roles in whiteface and singing a certain Irish song?

2. What actor's real name is Laszlo (Ladislav) Lowenstein? He is a German Jew, although he had been born in the Hungarian part of the Austro-Hungarian Empire.

3. This actor, who made his film debut at 61, was born in England and could trace his heritage back to the Norman Conquest, is _____ .

4. What character actor who had a 78 year film career (the longest in film history), played the pickpocket?

5. Who is the only cast member who had actually been to Casablanca?

6. In what was partly a publicity stunt, what 20 year old actress agreed to walk 5 miles a day each way to the studio, to symbolize sacrifice for the war effort?

7. What nickname did Jack Warner give to S.Z. Sakall who played Carl?

8. Jack Warner's niece by marriage was what 17 year old who played the role of Annina Brandel?

9. The ironic thing about Humphrey Bogart running a casino, a crooked one at that, is that he hated _____ .

10. Which actress was born Marie Therese Ernestine in Bourg La Reine, France on February 2, 1921?

11. Which actor, who plays a suave and urbane character, had only gone as far as the second grade and suffered from a serious cockney accent and speech impediment?

12. Which actor, who made his first film in 1941, earned an Academy Award nomination for *Casablanca*?

13. What actor had been born in Trieste, Austria-Hungary in 1908 and was the son of an aristocratic family that had connections to the banking business?

14. What actor finished his role in *Now Voyager* on June 3 and started his first scene in *Casablanca* at 10:30 AM on June 4?

15. What actor is a drinking friend of Humphrey Bogart, and was hired to replace another actor after the film had been in production for two weeks?

16. What German actor who played the role of the Free French member of the underground, later changed his name to Paul Andor?

17. Of all the actors who appeared in *Casablanca* which two were the only ones on the Warner Bros. contract list in 1942?

18. Which two key actors in the film never saw each other because one had finished his role before the other appeared on the set?

19. Which actor, whose career was on the rise before *Casablanca*, saw it decline after the thankless role that he played in *Casablanca*?

20. What actor was paid $2,267, but the money was wasted and none of his footage was used because he was replaced for not being funny enough?

21. Which actor in *Casablanca* got his start when his likeness was used in a baby food advertisement?

22. What two conditions did Paul Henreid get Warner Bros. to accept before he would agree to play the role of Victor Laszlo?

23. The three members of the 14 actors listed in the credited cast who were born in the United States were _____ .

24. Humphrey Bogart, Peter Lorre and Sydney Greenstreet had starred in what earlier film that helped make Bogart a star?

25. Ingrid Bergman's services in *Casablanca* were loaned by her studio to Warner Bros. for the services of what academy award winning actress?

26. The actor who was nominated for an academy award but claimed he had never seen the film is _____ .

27. Other than Ingrid Bergman, which two actors kissed Bogart in the film?

28. What actor completed his memorable role in only four days of shooting?

29. Because he had been gassed at Vilmy Ridge in WWI, what actor was almost blind in one eye?

30. What actor made substantial financial contributions to the British and Allied war effort, and through his many anti-Nazi films, became a symbol of resistance to the Nazis ?

Answers:

1. **Dooley Wilson**
2. **Peter Lorre**

3. Sydney Greenstreet
4. Curt Bois
5. Dooley Wilson
6. Madeleine Le Beau
7. "Cuddles"
8. Joy Page
9. gambling
10. Madeleine Le Beau
11. Claude Rains
12. Sydney Greenstreet
13. Paul Henreid
14. Claude Rains
15. Leonid Kinskey
16. Wolfgang Zilzer
17. Humphrey Bogart & Sydney Greenstreet
18. Peter Lorre & Paul Henreid
19. Paul Henreid
20. Leo Mostovoy
21. Humphrey Bogart
22. beef up the part and have equal billing with Bogart and Bergman
23. Humphrey Bogart, Dooley Wilson, Joy Page
24. *The Maltese Falcon*
25. Olivia de Haviland
26. Claude Rains
27. Leonid Kinskey & Joy Page
28. Peter Lorre
29. Claude Rains
30. Conrad Veidt

Factoid:

A horrific Pamela Anderson film *Barbed Wire*, is very loosely based on *Casablanca*.

"Two German couriers were found murdered in the desert.
The unoccupied desert. This is the customary roundup of refugees,
liberals, and uh, of course, a beautiful young girl for M'sieur Renault,
the Prefect of Police."

~ *The pickpocket* ~

Chapter 12
Film Makers &
Actors as Refugees

Many of the 34 nationalities participating in the making of
Casablanca were themselves refugees from Europe. The story of where
they came from and how they arrived in America is a fascinating
one that could be made into a documentary. The authenticity of the
performances, especially those in the minor roles, is due, in part, to the
fact that many of the actors had actually lived the roles of refugees.

Questions:

1. What St. Petersburg born actor left Russia at 17 after the
    October Revolution because he was part of a group who were not
    wanted by the ruling Communists?

2. This actor was a Triste born Austrian who went to England and
    could not return to his home in Vienna because of his anti-Nazi
    sentiments. He had been rounded up as an enemy alien in 1939
    when the war broke out between Germany and England. After
    coming to America he became a star leading man, he
    is _____ .

3. This actor, who like Richard Blaine left hours ahead of the invading German army, is what man who played the croupier in the film?

4. The usual path for film artists to get to Hollywood started in what city, and ended up in what country, before they arrived in Hollywood?

5. Which actor, who played Mr. Leuchtag, was imprisoned several times in German occupied Austria before he was able to escape and come to the Americas?

6. Which actor, who became a refugee himself with his second wife, made sure his daughter Viola and his first wife were safe in Switzerland, before he left for England to escape the Nazis?

7. 24 people who either acted in *Casablanca* or worked on the film were _____ .

8. What fate happened to the mother and father of the French actor Marcel Dalio, who was able to escape from Paris before the Germans arrived?

9. What group of refugees who contributed to the film, were not allowed to leave their homes between 8 PM and 6 AM because they were classified as "enemy aliens."

10. What refugee from Germany who played Heinze, had Americanized his name from Revy to get more roles?

11. What actor, who had been raised as a German in Germany, actually had been born in the United States while his parents were touring in Ohio; he did not realize this until after he became a refugee in Paris in 1933, and applied for a quota number to emigrate to the United States?

12. The technical advisor to *Casablanca* was what French army officer, who had escaped from a concentration camp and was the only refugee to follow the trail outlined in the film – from Paris to Marseilles, across the Mediterranean to Oran, to French Morocco (Casablanca), to Lisbon and then the new world?

13. Actors like Paul Henreid, Conrad Veidt, and Peter Lorre, who had starred in European films and had a better chance for success in Hollywood, were given what nickname (named after a dog)?

14. The reason Hans Twardowski (German officer who comes into the café with Yvonne) became a refugee, was not because he was Jewish but because he was a _____ .

15. Name the actor who played Annina's husband, Jan Brandel, who had been a leader of the anti-Nazi youth movement in Vienna.

16. Trudy Berlin, who played the woman at the baccarat table and asks if Rick will have a drink with her, is well known as what type of performer in Berlin before she became a refugee?

17. Name the actress who had 30 words in *Casablanca*; her background included playing Strindberg and Ibsen, as well as running the second-most important drama school in Berlin.

18. What refugee actor's photograph had been used on Nazi posters to demonstrate the features of a Jew?

19. After Hitler marched into Austria in 1938, what actor was sent to a concentration camp outside of Vienna for three months, before his influence and a friendly doctor got him released?

20. Before they became refugees, what 17 year old actress married a 40 year old actor, and they both had roles in *Casablanca*?

21. After WWI and the establishment of the counter-revolutionary Horthy regime in Hungary in 1919, what important creative force of *Casablanca* emigrated to the United States?

22. Which actor's second wife was Jewish, and after they were married he immediately emigrated from Germany to England to get her out of his home country?

23. After becoming a major star in Fritz Lang's *M,* what actor's satirical sense of humor got him into trouble with the new Nazi regime in Austria, which turned him into a refugee, by the Vienna-Paris route going first to England and then to the United States?

24. After they escaped from the Germans in Paris, Marcel Dalio and Madeleine Le Beau ended up coming to the Americas from what city in Europe?

25. Born in Bochum Germany in 1903, this actress had played stage roles at a prestigious theater in Darmstadt. She became a refugee, and after arriving in America, she received help from the European Film Fund. She is _____ .

26. After leaving Paris the night before the Germans arrived, what 19 year old spent three weeks crossing France to the Spanish border, and six weeks getting across Spain to Lisbon where she was joined by her husband?

27. After leaving Germany in 1933, what outspoken critic of the *Third Reich* returned in 1938 for a visit and the German government tried to keep him from leaving, saying he was too ill to travel. His British studio sent doctors that helped him get out of Germany. Who is he?

28. Marcel Dalio and Madeleine Le Beau left Lisbon with exit visas (unbeknownst to them these were fraudulent) for what country in South America, that they never reached because their freighter is diverted to Mexico?

29. When the pro-Axis government of Hungary gave all the Jews five days to get out of the country in 1939, who came to Hollywood with the help of a relative, producer Joe Pasternak?

30. What two refugee immigrants, who had bit parts in the film, fell in love and married in 1943, shortly after *Casablanca* is released?

Answers:

1. **Leonid Kinskey**
2. **Paul Henreid**
3. **Marcel Dalio**
4. **Berlin and England**
5. **Ludwig Stossel**
6. **Conrad Veidt**

7. refugees
8. died in concentration camp
9. Germans
10. Richard Ryan
11. Wolfgang Zilzer
12. Robert Aisner
13. St. Bernard
14. homosexual (gay)
15. Helmut Dantine
16. "cabaret"
17. Ilka Gruning
18. Marcel Dalio
19. Helmut Dantine
20. Madeleine Le Beau & Marcel Dalio
21. Michael Curtiz
22. Conrad Veidt
23. Peter Lorre
24. Lisbon
25. Lotte Palfi
26. Madeleine Le Beau
27. Conrad Veidt
28. Chile
29. S.Z. Sakall
30. Wolfgang Zilzer & Lotte Palfi

Factoid:

The Premiere of *Casablanca* at the Hollywood Theatre in New York City, was preceded by supporters of the Free French forces of Charles de Gaulle parading down 5th Avenue, and singing the "Marseillaise" as they unfurled the French flag at the theatre.

Factoid:

The most obvious goof or mistake in the film occurs as Rick is getting soaked in the rain at the Paris train station; but when he actually boards the train his raincoat is dry.

Factoid:

Dooley Wilson was borrowed from Paramount to play the role of Sam, but only $150 of his weekly check actually went to him as Paramount pocketed the rest of the $500 a week pay.

Factoid:

Ingrid Bergman was disappointed by Humphrey Bogart's standoff-ishness and said of their working relationship, "I kissed him but I never knew him."

Factoid:

Limousines that had routinely been used to transport stars and executives before the war, were replaced by jitney busses, demonstrating democracy in action as stars and executives traveled amongst the hairdressers, gaffers and other *hoi polloi*.

Factoid:

Lieutenant Casselle is haranguing Captain Tonelli about the Italian debacle in Greece, in which the Greeks with the help of the British, push the Italians back to Albania and are only rescued when the Germans enter and defeat the Greeks and push the British out. His point is that the Italians cannot win a battle without the Germans.

Factoid:

The entire film, except for the opening airport scene filmed at the Van Nuys Municipal Airport, was filmed at the Warner Bros.' Sound Stage in Burbank, California.

"Oh, we Germans must get used to all climates, from Russia to the Sahara."

~ Major Heinrich Strasser ~

Chapter 13
Places & Locations

Based on the un-produced play "Everybody Comes to Rick's," *Casablanca* has a surprising number of places and locations in the film. From the *Montmarte* to the Moorish quarter, there is much more to *Casablanca* than just Rick's *Café Americain*.

Questions:

1. The flashback scene takes place in what city in Europe?

2. The city of Casablanca is located in French colonial possession of _____ .

3. Where was Victor Laszlo being hidden on the outskirts of Paris?

4. What is the name of the café in Paris where Rick & Ilsa hear the news that the Germans will be in Paris the next day?

5. Sam and Rick leave Paris when they board the train at the *Gare de Lyon* that will take them to what city in southern France?

6. The boat ride that Rick and Ilsa enjoy in Paris takes place on what river?

7. In the opening of the flashback scene, what Paris landmark is shown?

8. What is the name of the café in the *Montmartre* district where Rick and Ilsa see each other for the last time in Paris?

9. Ferrari's Café, the center of all illegal activities in Casablanca where exit visas are sold, is the _____ .

10. The name of the lingerie shop in the *medina* outside of the Blue Parrot is _____ .

11. The "Clipper" is a plane that takes people from Lisbon to the _____ .

12. The specific location in Casablanca where the fishing "smack" (ketch) *Santiago* is going to leave from is _____ .

13. Most of the action in *Casablanca* takes place at Rick's Café, which is officially named _____ .

14. The opening long shot in the film shows the circular image of a _____ .

15. The opening scene is shot at what Southern California regional airport?

16. The three word inscription, *Liberte, Egalite, Fraternite* is carved into what building?

17. The office that Strasser uses in Morocco is the _____ .

18. Rick and Louis are going to incur 10,000 francs in expenses while traveling to what city in French Equatorial Africa?

19. The reason the Leuchtag's are only speaking English is so that they will feel at home when they reach _____ .

20. Name the two cities located in the Balkans where Strasser asks Laszlo to reveal the names of the underground leaders.

21. Which Paris café advertises *Liqueurs de Marque* and *Aperitifs* on its window sign?

22. In the opening scene, as the people look up at the arriving plane, they are milling around a location called the _____ .

23. The city that is located southwest of Casablanca on the map is _____ .

24. What runway is being used by the plane at the Casablanca airport that is going to Lisbon?

25. What place is Laszlo referring to when he sarcastically says to Strasser it "was honor enough for a lifetime?"

26. Which specific city is Rick referring to when he says "I bet they're asleep all over America?"

27. When Renault says that Strasser might find the climate in Casablanca a little warm, Strasser says Germans must get used to all kinds of climate from _____ .

28. What is the location in Casablanca where Berger tells Laszlo that the underground meeting will be held?

29. What is located in Brazzaville that Rick and Louis are going to join, in order to fight in the war against Germany?

30. A replica of what Paris landmark is sitting on the bar at *La Belle Aurora*?

Answers:

1. **Paris**
2. **Morocco**
3. **in a freight car**
4. *Café Pierre*
5. **Marseilles**
6. *Seine*
7. *Arc de Triumph*
8. *La Belle Aurora*
9. **Blue Parrot**
10. *Au Ron*
11. **Americas**
12. *La Medina*
13. *Café Americain*
14. **a globe or the world**
15. **Van Nuys**
16. *Palais de Justice*

17. **German Commissioner of Armistice**
18. **Brazzaville**
19. **America**
20. **Athens and Belgrade**
21. *Caffe Pierre*
22. *Defense Stationnaire*
23. **Mazagon**
24. **East**
25. **German concentration camp**
26. **New York**
27. **Russia to the Sahara**
28. *Caverne du Roi*
29. **a Free French garrison**
30. **Eiffel Tower**

Factoid:

During the filming, Paul Andor (member of the Resistance shot in the opening scene) and Lotte Palfi (women selling her jewelry) were courting and later were married.

Factoid:

The idea of taking the Clipper to America that Renault alludes to was a reality. The Pan American flight of a Boeing 314 luxury plane went from Lisbon to Bolama in Portuguise Guinea, and then across the Atlantic to Port of Spain, Trinidad, San Juan, Miami, and the trip finally ended at LaGuardia in New York City. Because of the favorable prevailing winds, the return trip was direct from New York to Lisbon non-stop.

"Of all the gin joints in all the towns in all the world, she walks into mine!"

~ Richard Blaine ~

Chapter 14
Rick

Humphrey Bogart landed the most memorable film role in history by playing Rick in *Casablanca*. Rick is the epitome of screen heroes with his snap-brim Fedora hat and his trench coat. He becomes the quintessential movie icon – much more than the sum of his parts.

Questions:

1. The actor that plays Rick in *Casablanca* is _____ .

2. Rick's full name is _____ .

3. How old is Rick in the film?

4. Where was Rick born?

5. What does Rick say to Louis that is the last line in the film?

6. What is Rick referring to when he says, "You played it for her, you can play it for me ...?"

7. What are the last words that Rick says to Victor and Ilsa at the airport?

8. The reason Rick gives for telling Ilsa that they will wait until the airport to tell Laszlo that Ilsa is staying with Rick, is that it will make it easier for all of us and give them _____ .

9. What does Rick give to Victor Laszlo to lesson the effects of the wound that Laszlo suffered, as he escaped from the police who raided the Resistance meeting?

10. Rick suggests to Ilsa that they can be married on the train to Marseilles by whom?

11. What is Rick's response to Renault's statement: "There is still something about the business I don't quite understand, Miss Lund, she's very beautiful, yes, but you were never interested in any women?"

12. What does Rick tell Ilsa that the only cause he is interested in is?

13. What does Rick reply to Ilsa's plea, "a free Laszlo will have his work and that he has been living for?"

14. What does Rick tell Ilsa not to bring up because it is poor salesmanship?

15. When Rick tells Carl that maybe he won't have to stay closed, what does he suggest they might do that had worked before?

16. What is Rick's verbal response to Annina when she hugs and kisses him after he helps Jan win at roulette?

17. What is Rick's response to Laszlo's speech that ends with "It's my privilege to be one the leaders of a great movement?"

18. What reason does Rick give to Laszlo for not selling him the "Letters of Transit" for any price?

19. What is Rick's answer to Annina's question about whether Renault will keep his word or not?

20. After Ilsa says "not tonight" when Rick says "I saved my first drink to have with you," Rick's two word response is

   _____ .

21. With the arrival of Victor Laszlo and Ilsa, what is the first precedent that Rick breaks, according to Renault?

22. Upon meeting Victor Laszlo, what does Rick congratulate him for?

23. What is Rick's answer to Strasser's question, "Who do you think will win the war?"

24. Complete the following line: "Who was it you left me for? Was it Laszlo, or were there others in between or _____ ?"

25. In talking to Ilsa at the lace sellers stand, what reason does Rick give for coming over to the Blue Parrot?

26. In answer to Strasser's question, what city does Rick say is not particularly his beloved one?

27. How much of the world has Laszlo succeeded in impressing according to Rick?

28. What is Rick's initial answer to Renault's question, "And what in heaven's name brought you to Casablanca?"

29. What interest does Rick tell Strasser he has in whether Laszlo stays or goes in Casablanca?

30. Rick says that as long as he has the "Letters of Transit" he will never be _____ .

Answers:

1. **Humphrey Bogart**
2. **Richard Blaine**
3. **37**
4. **New York City**
5. **"I think this is the beginning of a beautiful friendship."**
6. **"As Time Goes By"**
7. **"You better hurry, or you'll miss the plane."**
8. **"less time to think"**
9. **a drink (whiskey)**
10. **the engineer**
11. **"she isn't just any woman"**
12. **himself**
13. **"He won't have you."**
14. **Paris**
15. **a bribe**
16. **"He's just a lucky guy."**
17. **"The problems of the world are not in my department."**

18. "Ask your wife?"
19. "He always has."
20. "especially tonight"
21. has a drink with them (guests)
22. his work
23. "I haven't the slightest idea."
24. "aren't you the kind that tells."
25. To give Renault and Strasser a chance to ransack his place.
26. Paris
27. half
28. my health
29. a sporting
30. lonely

Factoid:

A recent rumor, that terrifies "*Casablancaistas,*" has Madonna starring in a remake of *Casablanca* to be filmed in Iraq.

Factoid:

The power of *Casablanca* as a romantic movie can be seen in a "Beverly Hills 90210" episode. After Dylan and Kelly watch the film Dylan cheats on Brenda.

Factoid:

When director Michael Curtiz is told that a scene makes no logical sense, his response is that he will "shoot it so fast no one will notice."

Factoid:

Curt Bois, who played the memorable role of the pickpocket in *Casablanca,* was once listed in the *Guinness Book of World Records* as having the longest film career in history – 78 years.

"We'll always have Paris. We didn't have it, we'd lost it, until you came to Casablanca. We got it back last night."

~ Richard Blaine ~

Chapter 15
More Rick

Has there ever been a character as rich in complexity and ambiguity as Richard (Rick) Blaine? The Bogart screen persona was perfect for the world-weary, cynical, tough guy with a heart of gold character of Rick. Underneath the seemingly impenetrable surface is a vulnerable idealist and romantic – if not a sentimentalist as Renault asserts.

Questions:

1. What game is Rick playing the first night in Casablanca before Ilsa arrives?

2. What does Rick do to the check that had been given to Sacha by the Germans?

3. The first four words Rick says in the film are _____ .

4. How does Rick describe Ferrari to Laszlo that would be politically incorrect today?

5. Where does Rick say he is settled and he invites Ilsa to come and see him, as he will be expecting her?

6. When Rick separates the French and German officers who are scuffling, what does he tell them to lay off of, or get out of his place?

7. Who tries to get Rick to take him into his confidence because he says Rick needs a partner?

8. What reason does Rick give to Ferrari for coming to the Blue Parrot in the morning?

9. When talking to Ilsa at the linen vendors Rick tells her that he is not doing what any more?

10. Besides Ilsa's story what else is it that had him confused the night before?

11. What snide remark does Rick make to Renault, in response to Renault admitting he has his orders to keep Laszlo in Casablanca?

12. Which employee of Rick's addresses him as *Herr Rick*?

13. How does Rick toast Ilsa when she says, "no questions," in response to his four questions?

14. What does Rick tell Ilsa had been "kicked out of him" as he waited on the train station platform for her?

15. The two slang terms that Rick uses to describe his *Café Americain* are _____ .

16. Who does Rick tell Renault to call off when he lets Laszlo go, because he does not want them around in the afternoon?

17. According to Rick the reason Renault lets him stay open is because Rick lets Renault _____ .

18. Where are Rick and Ilsa, and what are they doing, when Rick says "Here's looking at you, kid," the second time in the film?

19. What does Rick say in response to Louis' question, "Have you taken leave of your senses?"

20. The fact that Annina comes in with both her husband Jan, and Captain Renault, prompts Rick to say that Captain Renault is getting _____ .

21. Although Laszlo asks the band to play the "Marseilles," they do not play it until they get the OK from _____ .

22. What does Rick ask Carl to do because it might attract the police?

23. What is Rick's response to Renault's direct question, "have you got those 'Letters of Transit'?"

24. What sobriquet or nickname does Rick have for Ilsa?

25. What was Rick doing in June of 1930?

26. If he gave it any thought, what character would Rick despise?

27. Who is Rick referring to when he says they got a lucky break?

28. In selling his café to Ferrari, what does Rick remind Ferrari that he owes to Rick's?

29. What is the last thing Rick does when he gets on the train to Marseilles with Sam?

30. What does Rick do in his café when the flashback scene concludes, that Ilsa had done in the café in Paris?

Answers:

1. chess
2. tears it up
3. "Yes, what's the trouble?"
4. "the fat gent"
5. above a saloon
6. politics
7. Ferrari
8. to give Renault and Strasser a chance to ransack his place
9. running away
10. the bourbon
11. Gestapo spank
12. Carl
13. "Here's looking at you, kid."
14. his insides
15. gin joint and saloon
16. his watchdogs
17. win at roulette
18. drinking champagne at *La Belle Aurora*
19. I have

20. **broad minded**
21. **Rick**
22. **turn out the lights**
23. **Are you pro-Vichy or Free French?**
24. **kid**
25. **looking for a job**
26. **Ugarte**
27. **the two murdered German couriers**
28. **a hundred cartons of American cigarettes**
29. **throws away Ilsa's note**
30. **tips over a drink**

Factoid:

In writing a prequel to *Casablanca*, Michael Walsh suggested Sean Penn and Julia Roberts for the roles of Rick and Ilsa.

Factoid:

Upon reading the play, "Everybody Comes to Rick's," writer Robert Buckner derided Rick's character as being "two parts Hemingway, one-part Scott Fitzgerald, and a dash of café Christ."

Factoid:

The myth that Ronald Reagan was seriously considered for the role of Rick came from an announcement in the *Hollywood Reporter* on January 5, 1942 which said "Ann Sheridan and Ronald Reagan will be teamed by Warner Bros. for the third time in *Casablanca*, a story about war refugees in French Morocco." Dennis Morgan was also mentioned as one of the leads. There is no evidence that Reagan was ever considered and he was never approached for the role. The most likely explanation is that the announcement was a publicity stunt to keep Warner Bros. stars in the public eye.

"Was that cannon fire, or is it my heart pounding?"

~ Ilsa Lund ~

Chapter 16
Ilsa

What is remarkable about the character of Ilsa Lund, as played by Ingrid Bergman, is how few memorable lines she has; but how important her role is just the same. A look can be worth a thousand words, and the camera's work on Ilsa's face shows the emotional tumult of her role. Her furtive behavior when she first enters Rick's Café, the emotional transformation she displays as Sam plays "As Time Goes By" at her request, and when she buries her face on Bogart's shoulder, are all examples of her tremendous skill. Throughout the film, it is the feelings and emotions that she is able to display that make her performance so extraordinary.

Questions:

1. What actress played the role of Ilsa Lund?

2. What does Ilsa say the whole world is doing when she and Rick pick this time to fall in love in Paris?

3. When Ilsa holds a gun on Rick and asks him for the "Letters of Transit" where does she demand that he put the letters?

4. What city and country is Ilsa from?

5. What is Ilsa's response to Rick's question, "Why don't we get married in Marseilles?"

6. When does Ilsa say she will wear the blue dress again?

7. When Ilsa tells Rick she loves him so much at *La Belle Aurora*, what is it that she says she hates so much?

8. What are the final words that Ilsa says to Rick in Paris at the café?

9. The first time "As Time Goes By" is heard in the film is when _____ .

10. What name does Ilsa Lund call Rick in Paris?

11. What three things does Ilsa say Victor opened up a whole beautiful world for her?

12. What does Ilsa say in response to Rick's, "Here's looking at you, kid," the second night in Casablanca?

13. What is Ilsa's response to Rick's statement "Well, only one answer can take care of all our questions?"

14. What does Victor Laszlo always do for Ilsa in Rick's Café without consulting her, that many women today would find offensive?

15. Because Ilsa looked up to Victor Laszlo and worshipped him she supposed this was what sentiment?

16. What did Ilsa have done to herself ten years before meeting Rick in Paris?

17. What does Ilsa tell Rick he is taking out his revenge on, because one woman has hurt him?

18. What physical response does Ilsa do after Rick puts his arm around her while they are driving in the Paris flashback scene?

19. The character of Ilsa had what two last names in the film?

20. For playing Ilsa Lund in *Casablanca*, Ingrid Bergman's salary is _____ .

21. In the original stage play "Everyone Comes to Rick's," the name of the Ilsa Lund character is _____ .

22. While escaping from Europe, Ilsa Lund fell ill in what French city?

23. The last three words that Ilsa writes on the note to Rick just before her signature are _____ .

24. What prophetic line does Ilsa say to Rick after she tries to tell him a story, and he makes the sarcastic comment "Has it got a 'wow' finish?"

25. In what city in France did Ilsa have trouble getting out of, but Victor waited for her?

26. The reason Ilsa says that she and Victor kept their marriage a secret even from their closest friends was that it was a way of _____ .

27. After they have reconciled in Rick's room, what does Ilsa say Rick has to do for all of them?

28. In order to prepare for her role as Ilsa Lund and get familiar with Humphrey Bogart's acting style, Ingrid Bergman watched what Bogart film a number of times?

29. What does Ilsa first ask Sam to play when she talks to him the first night at Rick's?

30. What common term of endearment does Ilsa use to describe Rick?

Answers:

1. **Ingrid Bergman**
2. **crumbling**
3. **on the table**
4. **Oslo, Norway**
5. **"That's too far ahead to plan."**
6. **"When the Germans march out of Paris."**
7. **this war**
8. **"Kiss me as if it were the last time."**
9. **Ilsa hums it**
10. **Richard**
11. **knowledge, thoughts, ideals**
12. **"I wish I didn't love you so much."**
13. **"Well, only one question can take care of all questions."**

14. orders a drink for her
15. love
16. having a brace put on her teeth.
17. the rest of the world
18. puts her head on his shoulder
19. Lund and Laszlo
20. $25,000
21. Lois Meredith
22. Marseilles
23. "God bless you."
24. "I don't know the finish yet."
25. Lille
26. protecting her
27. think
28. *The Maltese Falcon*
29. some of the old songs
30. my darling

Factoid:

In 1982, film writer Chuck Ross retyped the screenplay to *Casablanca*, titled it "Everybody Comes to Rick's," and submitted it to 217 agencies dealing with film scripts. Of the 85 who read the material and responded, only 33 recognized the script; 38 rejected it; eight thought it sounded an awful lot like *Casablanca*; only three thought they could sell it; and one suggested turning it into a novel.

Factoid:

Ingrid Bergman's services had to be borrowed from David O. Selznick, who was paid $25,000 for letting her do *Casablanca* for a studio other than MGM. Bergman herself received $25,000 for the role. In order to clinch the deal, Olivia de Haviland was loaned from Warner Bros. to do a film for MGM.

"I am shocked, shocked to find that gambling is going on here!"
                                        ~ Captain Louis Renault ~

Chapter 17
Renault

What a character! Has there ever been a richer, more compelling supporting role than that of the womanizing, corrupt, amoral, caustic, ironic, cynical Chief of Police, Louis Renault. His role especially demonstrates how a character actor can bring such depth to a role that in Aljean Harmetz' words "(it) refracted the star's light so that formed a different and more complicated image. Rick's character would not have been as rich without the interplay between him and Renault." Renault's classic line, "I am shocked, shocked to find that gambling is going on in here!" as he collects his winnings, has become a metaphor for hypocrisy in our own time.

Questions:

1. The actor who starred as Louis Renault is _____ .

2. Louis Renault's official title in Casablanca is _____ .

3. Whenever a crime is committed what line does Renault say that becomes a *leit motiv* in the film?

4. Renault's least vulnerable spot is his

5. Claude Rains was nominated for what Academy Award for his performance in *Casablanca*?

6. What line does Renault use in the film in talking to Strasser; it is the title of the play *Casablanca* is based on?

7. What does Renault say that Rick is when it comes to women?

8. Renault's claim that "he blows with the wind" in terms of his beliefs is because he has no _____ .

9. Who is Renault referring to when he says that she may constitute and entire second front?

10. When Renault announces that Rick's is going to be closed; he says it will be closed until _____ .

11. Rick describes Renault to Annina as being just like any other man _____ .

12. What kind of business does Renault ask Berger about?

13. When ordered to close up Rick's Café by Strasser, what grounds does Renault use as his reason for closing it?

14. What does Renault say he would have to do to himself if he broke the curfew and is found drinking after hours?

15. What does Renault call Rick for helping Ethiopia in 1936?

16. Renault tells Rick that the influence of what German organization is over-estimated in Casablanca?

17. In Casablanca Renault claims he's master of his _____ .

18. Who is Renault referring to when he says he won't interfere with them, if they don't interfere with him?

19. What reason does Renault give for only being able to bet 10,000 francs with Rick, instead of the 20,000 that Rick suggests?

20. What does Renault decide to do at Rick's, instead of the Blue Parrot, to amuse Rick's customers because of his high regard for Rick?

21. On behalf of what government does Renault welcome Strasser to Casablanca?

22. In a double *entendre* Renault warns Strasser that he might find the climate in Casablanca a little _____ .

23. What honor does Renault say Laszlo will get for revealing the names and whereabouts of the leaders of the underground?

24. What is Rick's first reason why he might help Laszlo escape?

25. The type of hat worn by Renault in the film is called a
    _____ .

26. Although he is trying to cooperate with the German government Renault tells Strasser he cannot regulate the _____ .

27. What is Renault's second reason why Rick might help Laszlo's escape?

28. When Jan Brandel says he will be at Renault's office at 6:00 Renault responds that he will be at his office at _____ .

29. What is Renault's third reason why he thinks Rick might stick his neck out for Laszlo?

30. How many medals does Renault wear on his uniform?

Answers:

1. **Claude Rains**
2. **Prefect of Police**
3. **"round up the usual suspects"**
4. **heart**
5. **best supporting actor**
6. **"Everybody Comes to Rick's"**
7. **a true democrat**
8. **convictions**
9. **Yvonne**
10. **further notice**
11. **only more so**
12. **jewelry**
13. **there is gambling going on**
14. **fine himself**
15. **sentimentalist**
16. **Gestapo**
17. **fate**
18. **Gestapo**
19. **he is only a poor corrupt official**

20. **arrest the murderer of the couriers**
21. **Vichy or Unoccupied France**
22. **warm**
23. **having served the Third Reich**
24. **the 10,000 franc bet**
25. **kepi**
26. **feelings of the people**
27. **he has the "Letters of Transit"**
28. **10:00**
29. **he does not like Strasser's looks**
30. **three**

Factoid:

Claude Rains is the only member of the cast who never saw the completed film *Casablanca*.

Factoid:

Although he effortlessly portrayed an urbane Frenchman in *Casablanca*, in real life Claude Rains had to overcome a serious Cockney accent and speech impediment.

Factoid:

As a soldier in WWI, Claude Rains had been gassed at Vimy Ridge, which almost made him blind in one eye but he concealed it so no one knew.

Factoid:

In the Warner Bros. cartoon parody of *Casablanca* called *Carrotblanca*, Bugs Bunny played Rick, Daffy Duck played Sam, and Tweety Bird played Renault.

"If we stop breathing we'll die. If we stop fighting our enemies, the world will die."

~ Victor Laszlo ~

Chapter 18
Victor Laszlo

Of all the roles in the film the one character that has been criticized is Victor Laszlo. He is seen as 'stiff' for his rather wooden performance as a great leader of the Resistance. Although his character exudes a certain continental charm, his lack of passion causes viewers to have a negative view of the character.

Laszlo is not fiery enough to deserve Ilsa, nor is he charismatic enough to be a great leader. It is hard to see how he has "impressed the world" as Rick says. Despite these flaws, he does demonstrate a quiet strength that is best expressed in his leading of the singing of the "Marseilles."

Questions:

1. The actor who plays the role of Victor Laszlo is _____ .

2. Victor Laszlo is a leader of what organization?

3. What country had Victor Laszlo been a citizen of before it was absorbed into the Third Reich?

4. Twice Victor Laszlo had escaped from what German institution?

5. Laszlo loves Ilsa so much that he is willing to ask Rick what favor?

6. Besides being the leader of a cause, Victor Laszlo tells Rick that he is also a _____ .

7. What is it that Laszlo tells Rick he is trying to escape from, but he will never succeed?

8. What does Laszlo tell Rick to use to take Ilsa out of Casablanca?

9. What was it that Laszlo insisted be kept a secret, in order to protect Ilsa?

10. Laszlo believes that each person has a destiny to choose between which of two things?

11. When talking to Ilsa in the hotel room before going to the Resistance meeting, what does Laszlo call the man who has been following them?

12. According to Victor Laszlo being in a German concentration camp for a year was _____ .

13. Three times in the film Victor Laszlo orders a drink, and they are all different drinks that begin with the letter "C." What are they?

14. According to Victor Laszlo, who did Rick fight against in Spain?

15. Upon meeting Rick for the first time, what does Laszlo congratulate Rick for?

16. In response to a Strasser comment, what privilege does Laszlo sarcastically say he has never accepted?

17. How much will Victor Laszlo offer to anyone who will furnish him with an exit visa?

18. What is it that Ferrari tells Laszlo, that Laszlo already knows, because it becomes an instinct?

19. What kind of methods does Laszlo say the Germans had at their disposal in the concentration camps to force him to reveal the leaders of the underground?

20. What does Victor Laszlo do quite well in Casablanca, that no one is supposed to do well?

21. What does Victor Laszlo tell Rick will happen to the world if we quit fighting our enemies?

22. To drown out the German singing of *Watch on the Rhine* and show French patriotism, Victor Laszlo leads the patrons at Rick's in the singing of the _____ .

23. When Victor and Ilsa come into Rick's the second night, what request does Victor make that might prove to be a geographic problem?

24. Laszlo's friends in the underground told him of Rick's record of helping the _____ .

25. How many times does Victor kiss Ilsa on the cheek in their hotel room?

26. What drink does Victor order for himself and Ilsa, the second night at Rick's Café?

27. What does Victor Laszlo keep in the right hand outside pocket of his coat?

28. What type of drink does Laszlo order when he meets Berger at the bar, the first night at Rick's Café?

29. How long after *Casablanca* started filming did it take for Paul Henreid to appear on the set?

30. The reason that Paul Henreid did not step on the set of *Casablanca* until after it started filming, is because what picture he was starring in was running behind schedule?

Answers:

1. **Paul Henreid**
2. **Resistance**
3. **Czechoslovakia**
4. **concentration camp**
5. **take her out of Casablanca**
6. **human being**
7. **himself**
8. **"Letters of Transit"**
9. **their marriage**

10. good and evil
11. our faithful friend
12. honor enough for a lifetime
13. cointreaux, Champagne Cocktail, cognac
14. fascists
15. his interesting café
16. to be a subject of the German Reich
17. a fortune
18. that he is being shadowed (followed)
19. persuasive
20. sleep
21. it will die
22. "Marseilles"
23. a table close to Sam and as far away from Strasser as possible
24. underdog
25. two
26. cognac
27. cigarette case
28. Champagne Cocktail
29. one month
30. *Now Voyager*

Factoid:

In order to agree to the thankless role of Victor Laszlo, Paul Henreid insisted that he get equal billing with Bogart and Bergman as well as getting the girl in the end.

Factoid:

Before *Casablanca*, Paul Henreid was considered a rising star with romantic roles that emphasized his European charm. His was the only career that was harmed by the making of *Casablanca;* it went into decline and really never recovered after *Casablanca's* release.

"My dear Rick, when will you realize that in this world today isolationism is no longer a practical policy."

~ Signor Ferrari ~

Chapter 19
Strasser, Ugarte & Ferrari

As "heavies" go there is no finer trio than Major Heinrich Strasser, Ugarte, and Signor Ferrari. It is not screen time that matters only what is done with that time.

Instead of the usual heavy-handed stereotype of a Nazi, Major Strasser is a cultured, urbane, sophisticate, with a certain continental charm that masks his evil soul. In sparring with both Rick and Renault he is a worthy adversary, and his scenes with Victor Laszlo have just the right tone.

Ugarte's self-belittling comment, "What right do I have to think?" belies the more impressive aspect of Ugarte's personality – the murder of the two German couriers. His conversation with Rick is classic. As Rick insults him, Ugarte, in his oily, slimy way, turns the insults into something almost positive. Ugarte is the catalyst for the action in the film and his presence adds to its tension.

What can be said about Signor Ferrari, the respected and influential leader of all illegal activities in Casablanca? He realizes that isolationism is no longer a practical policy and that the buying and selling of human beings is Casablanca's leading commodity. With a suaveness that barely conceals his depravity, Ferrari could dismiss annoyances with the flick of his flyswatter. His presence sets much of the tone of intrigue in the film, and his vast girth makes the owner of the Blue Parrot's role much bigger than his lines or screen time.

Questions:

1. What actor, who was also in *The Maltese Falcon* with Humphrey Bogart and Sydney Greenstreet, played Ugarte?

2. Who played the role of Signor Ferrari?

3. Ferrari is the leader of what type of activities in Casablanca?

4. According to Ferrari, what is Casablanca's leading commodity?

5. Where is it that Strasser tells Ilsa, Laszlo must return to?

6. After the singing of the *Marseilles* drowns out *Watch on the Rhine,* who responds by ordering that Rick's be closed?

7. What do the *gendarmes* allow Ugarte to do before they place him under arrest?

8. Because he has the "Letters of Transit" who does Ugarte want to share his good luck with at Rick's?

9. In his conversation with Rick, what is it that Ugarte says he has no right to do?

10. What does Ugarte call the two dead German couriers?

11. When Ferrari tries to hire Sam away from Rick's, how much is he willing to pay Sam over what Rick pays him?

12. What does Ferrari say is no longer a practical policy in the world today?

13. Who does Ugarte bribe for his exit visa because it would be cheaper than getting it from Renault?

14. What reason does Ugarte give for only trusting Rick?

15. Rick does not mind that Ugarte is a parasite but he objects to him being a _____ .

16. The fact that he is the leader of all illegal activities in Casablanca makes Ferrari what kind of man?

17. What does Rick call Ferrari when he says, "You don't feel any sorrier for Ugarte than I do?"

18. What does Ferrari tell Laszlo that it will take to get him out of Casablanca?

19. What does Ferrari practically have a monopoly on in Casablanca?

20. According to Major Strasser what is human life worth in Casablanca?

21. What character's hair style is the "wet look" and has a prominent part on the right side?

22. A photo of what individual is hanging in Strasser's office?

23. The only character to smoke a cigar in the film is _____ .

24. Major Strasser's first name is _____ .

25. When Rick says, "one in, one out," the one out he is referring to is _____ .

26. What is Strasser doing when he shoots at Rick and Rick returns fire and kills him?

27. In response to Laszlo's inquiry about Ugarte, what is Strasser referring to when he tells Laszlo that the conversation would be a little one sided?

28. Strasser believes that Renault gives Rick too much credit for cleverness and calls him just another _____ .

29. Metaphorically, what animal does Strasser compare Laszlo to?

30. Who squeezes in the door when Rick is keeping the *Deutchesbank* representative out of his casino?

Answers:

1. **Peter Lorre**
2. **Sydney Greenstreet**
3. **all illegal ones**
4. **human beings**
5. **occupied France**
6. **Major Strasser**
7. **cash his chips**

8. his roulette wheel
9. think
10. poor devils
11. double his salary
12. isolationism
13. himself
14. because Rick despises him
15. cut rate one
16. influential and respected
17. a fat hypocrit
18. a miracle
19. black market
20. cheap
21. Ugarte
22. Adolph Hitler
23. Ferrari
24. Heinrich
25. Ugarte
26. calling the radio tower
27. Ugarte is dead
28. blundering American
29. the fox
30. Ugarte

Factoid:

In the unproduced play "Everybody Comes to Rick's" that *Casablanca* is based on, the character that becomes Ilsa Lund, is an unmarried American called Lois Meredith, who slept with three different men. Her character was changed, in part, because the Hay's Office in charge of the Hollywood Production Code, would never have approved of a woman with such loose morals.

"The leading banker in Amsterdam is now the pastry chef in our kitchen ... And his father is the bell boy."

~ Carl ~

Chapter 20
Rick's Employees

Despite Rick's cynical nature, during the early part of the film his basic decency can be seen in his relationship with his employees. When his café is closed down by Captain Renault, he keeps his staff on salary despite the fact he is not making any money. When he sells his café to Ferrari, he insists that his key employees stay with the place and Ferrari agrees that "Rick's wouldn't be Rick's without them." Sam, Abdul, Carl, Sacha, and Emil all play critical roles in the film.

Questions:

1. What two jobs does Carl have at Rick's?

2. What actor played Sam, the piano player and singer although he could not play the piano?

3. What song does Sam sing that becomes the most recognized song in the history of film?

4. Who played the nightclub singer in Rick's who was a trained coloratura soprano?

5. Sam advises Ilsa to leave Rick alone because she is _____ .

6. When asked if the gambling casino at Rick's is honest, Carl replies that it is as honest as the _____ .

7. Because he loves Yvonne, what is Sacha willing to do for her?

8. Who is Sacha referring to when he says "boom, boom, boom, boom, gave this check?"

9. What does Sacha do to Rick after he hears about what Rick did for the Brandels (Bulgarian couple)?

10. In the film, which employee tries to keep Rick from drinking by offering him coffee or water?

11. What three names does Sam call Rick in the film?

12. Which one of Rick's employees is a member of the Resistance?

13. Which employee of Rick's is in love with Yvonne?

14. Which character is the doorman to the casino at Rick's?

15. Which character is the croupier in the casino?

16. What is the name of the waiter, who seats Victor and Ilsa the second night in the café?

17. Which employee does Ferrari try to buy from Rick?

18. What percent of the profits at Rick's does Sam get?

19. In addition to Sam, what three employees will stay at Rick's when Ferrari takes over?

20. What reason does Sacha give for cutting off Yvonne from having any more drinks, despite the fact that he loves her?

21. What studio did Warner Bros. borrow Dooley Wilson from for his role as Sam?

22. What reason does Ferrari give for keeping Sacha, Abdul, and Carl at Rick's after he buys the café from Rick?

23. What character is the love-sick, demonstrative bartender who provides some comic relief in the film?

24. Dan Seymour, who played Abdul the doorman in the film, had a role in what other *Casablanca* film?

25. While Rick is getting drunk in his café the first night, what does Sam ask Rick, is Rick going to do in the near future?

26. What does Sam call Ilsa Lund in the film?

27. What two things does Sam suggest he and Rick should do instead of waiting around for Ilsa?

28. Which employee of Rick's celebrates with the older German couple who are going to America?

29. Because he anticipates that the older German couple are going to ask him to join him in their celebration, what two things does Carl bring to the table?

30. What is it that only employees drink at Rick's, according to Carl?

Answers:

1. **waiter and bookkeeper (accountant)**
2. **Dooley Wilson**
3. **"As Time Goes By"**
4. **Corinna Murra**
5. **bad luck**
6. **day is long**
7. **shut up**
8. **Germans**
9. **kisses him on both cheeks**
10. **Carl**
11. **Boss, Mr. Richard, Mr. Rick**
12. **Carl**
13. **Sacha**
14. **Abdul**
15. **Emil**
16. **Paul**
17. **Sam**
18. **10%**
19. **Sacha, Abdul, Carl**
20. **He (Rick) pays me**
21. **Paramount**
22. **Rick's wouldn't be Rick's without them**
23. **Sacha**

24. *A Night in Casablanca* (**Marx Brothers**)
25. **go to bed**
26. **Miss Ilsa**
27. **get drunk and go fishing**
28. **Carl**
29. **the good brandy and a glass for himself**
30. **the finest brandy**

Factoid:

The only member of the cast who had ever been to the city of Casablanca was Dooley Wilson (Sam) who had played a musical gig in that city before the war.

Factoid:

The proposed sequel to *Casablanca,* that was never made, was going to be titled *Brazzaville* after the capital of French Equatorial Africa, that Rick and Louis were headed to in order to join the Free French.

Factoid:

Dooley Wilson was a drummer/singer and could not play a note on the piano. The actual piano playing was by Elliot Carpenter (once considered for the role of Sam), as Wilson faked playing the songs on the piano.

Factoid:

One Warner Bros. executive objected to the title of *Casablanca* because it sounded too much like a Mexican beer (he was referring to *Carte Blanca*).

"Oh, M'sieur, you are a man. If someone loved you very much, so that your happiness was the only thing that she wanted in the world, but she did a bad thing to make certain of it, could you forgive her?"

~ Annina Brandel ~

Chapter 21
Minor Cast Members

Although many of the cast members who left Europe as refugees only landed minor roles in *Casablanca*, the richness of their performances in these minor roles made a major contribution to the film. Is there a better minor role in all of film history than Curt Bois' pickpocket?

Ludwig Stossel's Mr. Leuchtag and Ilka Grunig's Mrs. Leuchtag were only in one scene with Carl the waiter, but they made it a memorable one. High school student Joy Page, in her first acting role, has a key scene with Bogart that is perfectly underplayed.

One of the great strengths of the film is that the secondary or minor roles are done so well.

Questions:

1. Madeleine LeBeau, a 21 year old refugee, played what role in *Casablanca*?

2. What character, who is a member of the Resistance, invites Victor Laszlo to the meeting of the Underground at the *Caverne du Roi*?

3. What actor was still a high school student and only 17 years old when she made her film debut in *Casablanca*?

4. 56 year old Richard Ryan, who had changed his name from Revy, played what character in the film?

5. The Italian officer who tries to get a word in while arguing with the French officer is Captain _____ .

6. The character in the film who is Renault's aide, and never stops arguing with the Italian officer is _____ .

7. The older German couple, the Leuchtags, are celebrating with Carl because they are _____ .

8. What character in the opening scene, who has a key role in a later scene, says, "Perhaps tomorrow we will be on that plane?"

9. The actor John Qualen plays the role of what sympathetic character, who is a member of the Resistance?

10. The newly married couple, Jan and Annina Brandel, are escaping from what eastern European country where "a devil has the people by the throat?"

11. Joy Page, playing the role of Annina (the Bulgarian newlywed), was related to the head of Warner Bros.' Jack Warner in that she was his _____ .

12. Which actress in the film, who had a key but minor role, is married to Marcel Dalio, the croupier?

13. The announcer at the beginning of *Casablanca*, who has a Newsreel, "March of Time," type of voice is _____ .

14. Who played the character who reads the teletype tape into the phone announcing the murder of the two German couriers?

15. What character has the title of the German Consul in Casablanca?

16. What is ironic about Rick first offering Annina a drink in his café, and then recanting when he says, "No, you are under age?"

17. Rick's jilted mistress, whom he dumps even before Ilsa arrives is

_____ .

18. How does the Englishman say goodbye to the pickpocket in the opening scene?

19. What reason does the Arab linen seller have for giving the lady a small discount?

20. The Englishman describes the pickpocket in the opening scene as an _____ .

21. When Yvonne orders a whole row of drinks (French 75's), what does her date, the German officer, say they will start with?

22. What reason does Ferrari give to Rick for the fact that when he sends Rick's shipment over, it is always a little bit short?

23. What is it that Ferrari asks Rick to do that Rick says he never does in the morning?

24. What minor character says the scum of Europe has gravitated to Casablanca, which is ironic because he is actually describing himself?

25. What is Henri going to do with his champagne before he lets the Germans drink it?

26. What does Abdul call Carl which indicates what Carl's former profession was before becoming a waiter?

27. What is the pickpockets' signature line that he uses as he picks people's pockets in two different scenes?

28. What toast does Mr. Leuchtag offer that is repeated by Mrs. Leuchtag and Carl?

29. For special friends of Rick, how much is the Arab vendor willing to sell the tablecloth for?

30. What does Mr. Leuchtag ask Mrs. Leuchtag that violates their pledge to speak only English?

Answers:

1. **Yvonne**
2. **Berger**
3. **Joy Page**
4. **Heinze**
5. **Toneli**

6. Lieutenant Casselle
7. going to America
8. Annina (Bulgarian girl)
9. Berger
10. Bulgaria
11. his stepdaughter
12. Madeleine LeBeau
13. Lou Marcelle
14. Jean del Val
15. Heinze
16. Joy Page playing Annina was 17 and under age
17. Yvonne
18. *au revoir*
19. friends of Rick
20. amusing little fellow
21. two
22. carrying charges
23. have a drink
24. the pickpocket
25. water his garden with it
26. professor
27. "... this place is full of vultures, vultures everywhere, everywhere."
28. to America
29. 100 francs
30. what watch? (what time is it)

Factoid:

Although nominated for eight Academy Awards in 1943, *Casablanca* won only three, for Best Picture, for Best Screenplay, and Best Director.

"We hear very little, and we understand even less."

~ Englishman ~

Chapter 22
Production Staff

From the vision of producer Hal Wallis, to the deft directorial touch of Michael Curtiz, all of the production staff turned in exemplary performances under the Warner Bros. studio system.

The type of professionalism that existed at that time, led to a true collaborative effort to produce the best possible product, with limited funds (less than $1 million) and on a tight shooting schedule (59 days). *Casablanca*, which has been called the "happiest of happy accidents," came together in spite of misgivings about the unfinished script and other issues.

Questions:

1. What veteran director, a Hungarian expatriate, won an Oscar for directing *Casablanca*?

2. What role did Hal Wallis play in making *Casablanca*?

3. Art Silver was the creator of what two minute and 12 second marketing tool for *Casablanca*?

4. Who wrote the play, "Everybody Comes to Rick's" that was the basis for the film?

5. Which one of the writers of *Casablanca* is responsible for the political tension and much of the anti-fascist political slant of the film?

6. The cinematographer for *Casablanca*, whose filming emphasizing the story and the actors, is today seen as one of the greatest strengths of the movie is _____ .

7. What is the name of the 35 year old story reader who, while making $1.12 an hour, was the first person to read the play, "Everybody Comes to Rick's," and recommended that it be bought to be made into a movie?

8. What was the name of the writing team of brothers who contributed the humor, wit, bravado, sarcasm, and cynicism to the script?

9. Who was the independent producer who controlled the contract of Ingrid Bergman, and charged $75,000 for her services in *Casablanca* in which she received $25,000?

10. The member of a famous family of make-up artists who was responsible for the make-up in *Casablanca* is _____ .

11. The veteran German expatriate art director who had already done *The Adventures of Robin Hood* and *Yankee Doodle Dandy* is _____ .

12. Which one of the writers for *Casablanca* ended up accepting the Oscar for Best Screenplay?

13. Which director was Hal Wallis' original first choice, but could not do the film because he was tied up with another project?

14. The driving force behind *Casablanca* and all Warner Bros.' projects was which Warner brother?

15. The studio manager in charge of technicians, who had enough power under the Warner Bros. system to keep Hal Wallis from getting the cameraman he wanted is _____ .

16. Who is the hairdresser who did Ingrid Bergman's hair in the film, but because there was no setting of the hair or bobby pins used, most of her work consisted of the constant brushing of Bergman's hair?

17. Hal Wallis' favorite screenwriter who is brought into the project to shape the love story between Rick and Ilsa is _____ .

18. The head of the story department at Warner Bros. who used her considerable influence to get the studio to buy the play "Everybody Comes to Rick's" is _____ .

19. The sound editor of *Casablanca* who is berated on the first day of shooting by director Michael Curtiz is _____ .

20. The Assistant Director of *Casablanca* who would later be one of the founders of the Directors Guild of America is _____ .

21. Which writing team worked on the script of *Casablanca* for seven weeks, but none of their material is ever used?

22. The musical director of *Casablanca*, who in a long career would be nominated for 26 Academy Awards (including *Casablanca*) and win three Oscars is _____ .

23. Two writers that Hal Wallis considered for writing the script, who were ultimately rejected because they were working on other projects are _____ .

24. The cameraman that Hal Wallis wanted to film *Casablanca* who was not available because the studio manager would not take him from another project is _____ .

25. What writing partner of Murray Burnett is credited with being the co-writer of the play "Everybody Comes to Rick's?"

26. Much of the natural look of the film is credited to the work of what costume designer?

27. The creator of the set decorations in *Casablanca* is _____ .

28. The cutting for *Casablanca* is done by what veteran film editor, who had worked earlier on *Disraeli* and *The Private Lives of Elizabeth and Essex*?

29. The opening montage scene is created by what future director of *Invasion of the Body Snatchers* and *Dirty Harry*?

30. Which member of the production staff is responsible for the name change from "Everybody Comes to Rick's" to *Casablanca*?

Answers:

1. **Michael Curtiz**
2. **Producer**
3. **Trailer**
4. **Murray Burnett**
5. **Howard Koch**
6. **Arthur Edeson**
7. **Stephen Karnot**
8. **Epstein (Philip & Julius)**
9. **David O. Selznick**
10. **Perc Westmore**
11. **Carl Jules Weyl**
12. **Howard Koch**
13. **William Weyler**
14. **Jack**
15. **T.C. Tenny Wright**
16. **Jean Burt**
17. **Casey Robinson**
18. **Irene Lee**
19. **Francis Scheid**
20. **Lee Katz**
21. **McKenzie & Klein**
22. **Max Steiner**
23. **Lenore Coffee & Arch Oboler**
24. **James Wong Howe**
25. **Joan Alison**
26. **Orry Kelly**
27. **George James Hopkins**
28. **Owen Marks**
29. **Don Siegel**
30. **Hal Wallis**

"As leader of all illegal activities in Casablanca, I am an influential and respected man."

~ *Signor Ferrari* ~

Chapter 23
Actors Considered
for Casablanca Roles

The number of actors whose names were floating around for possible roles in *Casablanca* is an incredibly long list. Some were seriously considered and were actually screen tested, but most were just rumors or publicity stunts.

For example, singers, actors, and musicians as diverse as Lena Horn, Hazel Scott, Elliot Carpenter, Charles Muse, Ella Fitzgerald, William Gillespie, Napoleon Simpson, Fred Skinner and ultimately Dooley Wilson, were all considered for the role of Sam.

In addition, numerous actors were considered for most of the other roles including Rick, Ilsa, Victor as well as many of the supporting roles.

Questions:

1. The best example of an actor whose name is mentioned as possibly getting the leading role in *Casablanca*, is what "B" actor who would later became famous for another occupation?

2. Jack Warner mentioned the name of which "tough guy" actor for the role of Rick, but his suggestion is never seriously considered by producer Hal Wallis?

3. Louis B. Mayer, chief executive at MGM, refused to loan out which actress, who had starred in *Algiers* – the film that was the model for *Casablanca* – for a screen test in *Casablanca* for the role of Ilsa?

4. What actor, who later became a famous Hollywood director of such films as *Porgy and Bess, Anatomy of a Murder,* and *Exodus,* is screen tested for the role of Major Strasser?

5. What female black singer, known as the "first lady of song," is briefly considered for the role of Sam by the producers of *Casablanca*?

6. What actor, nicknamed the oomph girl, who had appeared in *Angels Have Dirty Faces* and *Kings Row*, is first mentioned for the role of Ilsa?

7. What star of *Citizen Kane* and *The Magnificent Ambersons,* is briefly considered for the role of Victor Laszlo, but the asking price of $25,000 to borrow him from David O. Selznick is too high?

8. What French actor and war hero, who starred in *Day for Night, Maria Chapdelaine,* and *Vacances Portugaises,* is screen tested for the role of Victor Laszlo?

9. Although his name is floated as being in *Casablanca*, what actor is never seriously considered for the role of Rick, because he is a Second Lieutenant in the U.S. Calvary Reserve and Warner Bros. knew he would soon be called up for duty?

10. What French actress, who asked for $55,000, actually tested for the role of Ilsa, but the producers became turned off on her because of her excessive asking price?

11. One of the founders of the Black Theatre Company, who was originally favored for the role of Sam by the producer Hal Wallis, and was rejected because his acting style is considered to be too stereotypical is _____ .

12. After seeing the movie *Sarajevo*, Producer Hal Wallis thought what star, known as the "first lady of the French screen," would be ideal for the role of Ilsa if she could speak any English?

13. Wallis' initial choice for the Victor Laszlo role, is which Dutch actor who had played the leader of Germany's anti-Nazi movement in the Warner Bros.' film *Underground*?

14. Two actors with English accents who are considered for the role of Victor Laszlo but are second choices to Paul Henreid and Phillip Dorn are _____ .

15. Hal Wallis, in his quest to give the role of Sam to a woman, considered what performer because he admired her act at the Uptown Café Society Club in New York City?

16. What pianist tested for the role of Sam, did not get the part, but actually played the piano while Dooley Wilson did his "air piano" act for the playing of songs in the film?

17. The two primary writers of *Casablanca*, the Epstein Brothers, were unhappy with the casting of what actor because he was English and they thought a French actor should have the role?

18. William Gillespie, Napoleon Simpson, and Fred Skinner, all screen tested for what role that tried out more performers than any other role in the film?

19. Mikhail Rasumny and Michael Delmatoff are both considered for the role of the bartender that is given to Leo Mostovoy, who is replaced by _____ .

20. Hal Wallis was willing to accept what actor for the role of Ferrari, if Sydney Greenstreet could not be persuaded to play the role?

21. The actor who was first cast as the Russian bartender Fydor by Director Michael Curtiz, and was replaced by Hal Wallis because he was not funny, and wrong for the part is _____ .

22. The first publicity for *Casablanca* in the *Hollywood Reporter*, mentions what actor (he had appeared in *Kitty Foyle* and *The Fighting 69th*) after the co-stars, as one who should come in for top billing?

23. A Mexican screen siren who was known for her sexy outfits in the Spanish version of *Dracula*, who is briefly considered for the role of Yvonne is _____ .

24. Screenwriter Casey Robinson changed the nationality of American Lois Meredith in the play, to a European because he wanted to shape the role for what Russian ballerina who infatuated him?

25. George Tobias, who would later star on television's "Bewitched" as next door neighbor Abner Kravitz, is considered for what small role in *Casablanca* that is difficult to fill?

26. For the role of Victor Laszlo, Hal Wallis tried to get what actor who had played the role of an Oriental warlord, to Barbara Stanwyck's missionary, in *The Bitter Tea of General Yen*?

27. A character type actor whom Wallis was willing to settle for, if he could not get a major star for the Laszlo role, is what actor who appeared in 120 films in his career and later won an Oscar for Best Supporting Actor in *Twelve O'Clock High*?

28. Stephen Karnot, the reader who first recommended the play "Everybody Comes to Rick's" be made into a movie, suggested what actress, who had starred with Bogart in *The Maltese Falcon*, for the female lead?

29. What suave and debonair Viennese actor with a pencil-slim moustache, who had fled the Nazis, is also considered for the role of Victor Laszlo?

30. Hal Wallis considered what beautiful, light-skinned, black singer for the role of Sam, but she is not available for *Casablanca* because she had just been placed under contract to MGM?

Answers:

1. Ronald Reagan
2. George Raft
3. Hedy Lamar
4. Otto Preminger
5. Ella Fitzgerald
6. Ann Sheridan
7. Joseph Cotton
8. Jean Pierre Aumont
9. Ronald Reagan
10. Michelle Morgan
11. Charles Muse
12. Edwige Feuillere
13. Philip Dorn
14. Ian Hunter & Herbert Marshall
15. Hazel Scott
16. Elliot Carpenter
17. Claude Rains
18. Sam
19. Leonid Kinskey
20. J. Edward Bromberg
21. Leo Mostovoy
22. Dennis Morgan
23. Lupita Tovar
24. Tamara Toumanova
25. Fydor or Sacha
26. Nils Asther
27. Dean Jagger
28. Mary Astor
29. Carl Esmond
30. Lena Horn

Factoid:

Although he despised gambling, Bogart was passionate about chess because there is no luck to it. During the filming of *Casablanca*, the chess scenes were an actual game that he was playing with Irving Kovner of Brooklyn, New York.

Factoid:

Screenwriter Casey Robinson changed the role of the female lead from an American to a European, because he was infatuated with Russian actress Tamara Toumanova and he wanted to shape the role for her. She tested for the role but did not get it.

Factoid:

Casablanca went into general release on January 23, 1943, just as Franklin Roosevelt and Winston Churchill were finishing their famous conference in the city of Casablanca.

Factoid:

In order to promote the war effort, Warner Bros. announced that 21 year old actress Madeleine LeBeau (Yvonne) would be walking five miles each way to the studio for work.

Factoid:

The largest French colony to join Charles De Gaulle in opposing the Germans and the Vichy regime was French Equitorial Africa, with Brazzaville as its capital. It was a logical choice for Rick and Louis to flee to.

"You played it for her and you can play it for me. If she can stand it, I can. Play it!"

~ Richard Blaine ~

Chapter 24
Influences, Imitators
& Sequels

From Woody Allen's misnamed film *Play It Again Sam,* to Warner Bros.' own *Carrotblanca* starring Bugs Bunny as Rick, there have been many "take-offs," parodies, inspired imitators and other influences of *Casablanca* in film and popular culture. There has been constant speculation about a remake over the years, but so far no one has had the gall to try it. The latest scuttlebutt is a Bollywood version from India. It is also rumored that the pop-icon Madonna is interested in a remake of *Casablanca.*

Questions:

1. The proposed name for the sequel to *Casablanca* is what city located in French Equatorial Africa?

2. A 1982 song by Bertie Higgins had the lyric "Here's looking at you kid." However, the song title and most of the content is from what different Bogart film?

3. Which item is often sold in stores, that is so associated with the film that it is sometimes just called a Casablanca?

4. Which Academy Award winning actress was going to star in the sequel to *Casablanca* as a Red Cross nurse?

5. Which film, with a European city in its title, is an attempt to duplicate the success of *Casablanca* by reuniting its producer, director, and four of the principle actors?

6. What actor played the role of Rick on the Lux Radio Theatre version of *Casablanca* in 1944?

7. What Canadian figure skater emulated Rick in his attire, attitude, and program, and skated to the music of *Casablanca* in winning the 1993 World Skating Championship?

8. In the 1955 TV series *"Casablanca,"* Sydney Greenstreet's role of Signor Ferrari is taken by what actor who had a small role as one of Rick's employees in the original *Casablanca*?

9. The second attempt at a *Casablanca* television series, starred what actor who had made a name for himself in the TV series *"Starsky and Hutch?"*

10. What host of *"Saturday Night Live"* played Ilsa in a memorable skit with John Belushi who played Rick?

11. What 1945 Howard Hawks film, had many of the same elements as *Casablanca* except the female lead introduced Lauren Bacall to Bogart?

12. Woody Allen's play and later film, immortalized what line that is attributed to, but never said, in *Casablanca*?

13. What actor who had been one of Rick's employees in the original *Casablanca*, is promoted to Captain Renault's role in the Warner Bros. T.V. series?

14. Gravel voiced, *film noir* veteran actor, who starred as Rick in the first attempt of a *"Casablanca"* TV program in 1955 is

_____ .

15. What European actress, who had been considered for the role of Ilsa, finally got to play the part on the Lux Radio Theatre?

16. What 1990 Sydney Pollack movie starring Robert Redford and Lena Olin, reused many elements from *Casablanca*?

17. What well known actor and the star of *Goodfellows*, played the role of Sacha in the 1983 TV series of *"Casablanca?"*

18. In 1987, an unauthorized version of *Casablanca* that had been re-cut from the original, only with the happy ending of Ilsa going with Rick, is shown at what South American film festival?

19. What cartoon character starred as Rick in Warner Bros.' cartoon parody of *Casablanca*?

20. In the Warner Bros. cartoon version of *Casablanca*, who played the role of Renault?

21. What is the name of the Warner Bros.' cartoon version of *Casablanca*?

22. In the cartoon version of *Casablanca*, the role of Sam is played by _____ .

23. What title does Michael Walsh give to his 1998 prequel to *Casablanca*?

24. In his 1998 book, Walsh suggests what two actors for the roles of Rick and Ilsa?

25. What actor does Michael Walsh mention for the role of Victor Laszlo in his prequel to *Casablanca*?

26. What 1988 film, named after a cocktail, starring Mel Gibson, Kurt Russell, and Michelle Pfeiffer tried to bill itself as the *Casablanca* of the 1980's?

27. A 1980 film directed by J. Lee Thompson which has a look alike title and is a *Casablanca* pastiche set in a fishing village on the Peru coast is _____ .

28. What prominent character actor played Renault in the short-lived 1983 *"Casablanca"* TV series?

29. What 1990s horror film (sequel) announced that *Casablanca* would be recast in full color with a happy ending?

30. Who played Sam in the 1983 TV version of *Casablanca*?

Answers:

1. **Brazzaville**
2. **"Key Largo"**
3. **ceiling fan**
4. **Geraldine Fitzgerald**
5. *Passage to Marseilles*
6. **Alan Ladd**
7. **Curt Browning**
8. **Dan Seymour**
9. **David Soul**
10. **Candace Bergman**
11. *To Have and Have Not*
12. *Play it Again Sam*
13. **Marcel Dalio**
14. **Charles McGraw**
15. **Hedy Lamar**
16. *Havana*
17. **Ray Liotta**
18. **Rio**
19. **Bugs Bunny**
20. **Tweety Bird**
21. *Carrotblanca*
22. **Daffy Duck**
23. *As Time Goes By*
24. **Sean Penn & Julia Roberts**
25. **Ralph Fiennes**
26. *Tequila Sunrise*
27. *Caboblanca*
28. **Hector Elizondo**
29. *Gremlins 2: The New Batch*
30. **Scatman Crothers**

"Well, I told Strasser he wouldn't find the letters here. But I told my men to be especially destructive. You know how that impresses Germans?"

~ Louis Renault ~

Chapter 25
Awards, Honors,
Cults & Fads

For a film to be considered really memorable it must inspire something beyond the film itself. From its many quoted lines, its influence on fashion, and its general standing as a cultural icon, *Casablanca* represents much more than just another WWII film.

Over the years *Casablanca* has stood the test of time in garnering up honors and awards. This popularity is not just in the United States, but is world wide. To paraphrase Rick's comment to Victor Laszlo, "One hears a great deal about *Casablanca* everywhere."

Questions:

1. In 1943, *Casablanca* is nominated for how many Academy Awards?

2. In what year did *Casablanca* win the Academy Award for Best Picture?

3. How many Academy Awards did *Casablanca* win?

4. In 1983, which foreign film organization named *Casablanca* the best film of all time?

5. Which fashion trend did Bogart start, regarding the wearing of the trench coat in the airport scene?

6. Although it is memorable today, Max Steiner's music score for *Casablanca* lost the Academy Award to what film's music score?

7. The American Film Institute's 1970s survey of the greatest American films ranked *Casablanca* as _____ .

8. Charles Coburn won the Oscar as Best Supporting Actor for *The More the Merrier,* beating out what nominated actor from *Casablanca*, in what is considered one of the greatest injustices in the history of the Academy Awards?

9. The death of what actor in 1957, is the catalyst for the beginning of the *Casablanca* cult that started three months later?

10. What university is credited with starting the *Casablanca* cult by featuring Bogart festivals during finals week?

11. The start of the *Casablanca* cult and Bogart festivals began at what art-house movie theatre in what city in 1957?

12. In what country in central Europe is *Casablanca* traditionally shown on New Year's Eve?

13. What TV publication has said that *Casablanca* is both the most requested and film most shown on television?

14. The director of *Casablanca* who won the Academy Award is _____ .

15. Two items of clothing that Bogart wears in *Casablanca* that not only become his signature, but also become cultural icons are _____ .

16. In a survey of the top 100 lines from all films, *Casablanca* has how many lines listed, which is more than any other film?

17. In 2001, the Writers Guild of America voted the screenplay for *Casablanca* what ranking out of "101 Greatest Screenplays?"

18. In 1989, *Casablanca* was selected along with 24 other films for preservation, as being deemed "culturally, historically, or aesthetically significant" by what organization?

19. In 2002, the American Film Institute gave *Casablanca* what ranking in the "100 Greatest Love Story (Romance) Films of All Time?"

20. What ranking did Rick (Richard Blaine) have in the American Film Institutes' 2002 list of the "Greatest Film Heroes of All Time?"

21. In terms of the "100 Greatest Song Rankings" from the American Film Institutes' 2002 list, "As Time Goes By" is ranked

    _____ .

22. In its list of the 100 top "Romance Movies of All Time," the modern website AOL's Moviefone lists *Casablanca* as

    _____ .

23. The documentary movie, *Casablanca Revisited*, a homage to *Casablanca* and the films of the 1940s, is awarded the best short movie in what International Film Festival in Spain in 1992?

24. In 1988, a poll of 22 of the world's top movie critics on the all-time popularity of 100 famous movies, *Casablanca* is ranked

    _____ .

25. The scene with Rick and Ilsa on the tarmac at the airport, is chosen as the Most Romantic Scene in Movie History by what organization in 2001?

26. The "Casablanca Award" is the most coveted award at which film festival honoring independent films, that started in 2002?

27. During the 1960s when *Casablanca* became a cult classic, it was often shown on college campuses or nearby theatres during what stressful time for students?

28. Although no scientific survey is known to exist, by anecdotal evidence, *Casablanca* is the film that is most frequently shown in what institutional setting?

29. The *Casablanca* name has so much *cache* that the Rocky Mountain Education Services have named their educational program the _____ .

30. The complexity and popularity of *Casablanca* has resulted in a 1,130 question trivia book about all aspects of the film, and its title is _____ .

Answers:

1. 8
2. 1943
3. 3
4. British Institute of Film
5. tying, not buckling, the belt of his trench coat
6. *The Song of Bernadette*
7. #3
8. Claude Rains
9. Humphrey Bogart
10. Harvard
11. Brattle in Cambridge, Massachusetts
12. Hungary
13. *T.V. Guide*
14. Michael Curtiz
15. snap brim fedora hat and trench coat
16. 6
17. 1
18. National Film Registry
19. 1
20. 4
21. 2
22. 1
23. Gijón
24. 9
25. Cosmique Movie Awards
26. Lake Havasu Film Festival
27. Finals week
28. college film classes
29. American Academy of Casablanca
30. *Casablanca Film Trivia: "Here's Looking at You, Kid!"*

"It can be most helpful to know Signor Ferrari. He's pretty near got a monopoly on the black market here."

~ *Native* ~

Chapter 26
History of the Film

As this book can attest, there is a thriving industry that just focuses about the making and the meaning of the film *Casablanca*. Ten complete books have been written about the history of the making of the film, and scores of articles written by film scholars and critics have been produced over the years. Although it is 65 years old and in black and white, there is still as much interest in *Casablanca* as any film ever made.

Questions:

1. What two political leaders were meeting in Casablanca when the film was placed in general release in January of 1943?

2. The Office of War Information was uneasy about the negative portrait of what European government in *Casablanca*?

3. Because of the impetus from *Casablanca*, Bogart replaced what actor as the #1 star for Warner Bros.?

4. Instead of *Casablanca,* what 1943 film won most of the critics' awards?

5. Humphrey Bogart followed up his role in *Casablanca* with what successful WWII film that took place on the ocean?

6. In 1947 one of the writers of *Casablanca*, Howard Koch, would be one of 19 unfriendly witnesses subpoenaed by what Congressional committee that was looking for communists?

7. Paul Henreid had to be borrowed from what studio to star in *Casablanca*?

8. The U.S. government agency that kept *Casablanca* from being shipped to North Africa for overseas showing is the _____ .

9. Ludwig Stössel, who played Mr. Leuchtag, later became famous for playing a little old wine maker in what television commercial?

10. Rick's Café was modeled after what hotel in Tangiers?

11. What military and political leader in WWII requested that *Casablanca* be shown to his troops?

12. In what western European country, not controlled by or an ally of the Third Reich, was *Casablanca* banned from being shown during WWII?

13. Warner Bros. boasted that how many people of different nationalities were involved in the making of *Casablanca*?

14. *Casablanca* is released in January of 1943, to avoid having to compete against what Academy Award winning picture with a WWII setting that had been released in December of 1942?

15. In 1946, *Casablanca* is shown in Germany, but to comply with new laws it was a truncated version, primarily because what prominent word from the film is expunged?

16. What did the promotional liners on the original playbill say about *Casablanca*?

17. The official sponsor of the 50th Anniversary Edition of *Casablanca* was what commercial beverage?

18. On Tuesday September 22, 1942, *Casablanca* is previewed at theatres in what two suburbs of Los Angeles?

19. In the video version of *Casablanca* what rating did it receive?

20. What company is the current owner of *Casablanca*?

21. What well known company published a calendar based on the film *Casablanca* in 1997 that sold for $10.95?

22. In Jean Luc Goddard's *Breathless*, the petty crook who stops in front of a Bogart movie poster and tries to imitate both he and his generation's idol, is played by what well known French actor?

23. When *Casablanca* is shown after WWII in Europe, what country besides Germany are Major Strasser and all the references to the Nazis cut entirely from the film?

24. In 1987, what vehicle used in *Casablanca* is purchased from a crop duster to be used in the "Great Movie Ride" attraction at Disney World in Orlando, Florida?

25. What comedic actors spoofed *Casablanca* in 1946 with the release their film, *A Night in Casablanca* about a Nazi spy ring operating out of a North African hotel and night club?

26. After the release of *A Night in Casablanca,* Jack Warner ordered his attorneys to _____ .

27. What comedy series with a mostly black cast, did its version of the film with Marla Gibbs as Ilsa, Hal Williams as Rick, and singer-songwriter Paul Williams as Sam?

28. Upon receiving his Academy Award for *Casablanca*, whose memorable acceptance speech, which was characteristic of his use of English in general, said, "So many times I have a speech ready, but no dice. Always a bridesmaid, never a mother?"

29. What man successfully defended himself against a lawsuit by Murray Bennett and Joan Alison for writing in his biography, *Bogie,* " 'Everybody Comes to Rick's,' died before it ever reached Broadway?"

30. Which item pertaining to the promotion of *Casablanca* has been recently auctioned off by Sotherby's for $35,000?

Answers:

1. **Churchill and Roosevelt**
2. **Unoccupied France or Vichy France**
3. **Errol Flynn**
4. ***Watch on the Rhine***

5. *Action in the North Atlantic*
6. HUAC (House Un-American Activities Committee)
7. RKO
8. Office of War Information
9. Italian Swiss Colony Wine
10. El Minzah
11. Charles de Gaulle
12. Ireland
13. 34
14. *Mrs. Miniver*
15. Nazi
16. "They had a date with fate ... in a city that rocked the world."
17. Taster's Choice Coffee
18. Pasadena & Huntington Park
19. PG
20. Turner Broadcasting (a subsidiary of AOL-Time Warner)
21. Hallmark
22. Jean Paul Belmondo
23. Sweden
24. Lockheed Electra 12A (airplane taking off at the end of the film)
25. Marx Bros.
26. get the name *Casablanca* out of the title
27. "227"
28. Michael Curtiz
29. Nathaniel Benchley
30. an original movie poster

Factoid:

Black female singers Lena Horn and Ella Fitzgerald were briefly considered for the role of Sam along with a number of other singers.

"Each of us has a destiny, for good or for evil."

~ Victor Laszlo ~

Chapter 27
Behind the Scenes

Many books have been written about the making of *Casablanca* from the perspective of "behind the scenes." The story of what happened during the making of the film, decisions made about the film, and actions of the participants have been richly described by Aljean Harmetz in *Round Up the Usual Suspects,* Frank Miller in *As Time Goes By,* Harlan Lebo in *Casablanca Behind the Scenes,* Charles Francisco in *You Must Remember This: The Filming of Casablanca,* Richard Osborne in *The Casablanca Companion,* and *The Casablanca Companion* by Jeff Siegel.

Questions:

1. For most of the time *Casablanca* is being filmed, what writer was writing behind the Epstein Brothers and revising their work?

2. While filming is going on, what actor filed for divorce against his wife who was also in the film, on the grounds of desertion?

3. Although only on the set for four days what actor had the set in a uproar by his antics?

4. What prominent actor known for his "tough guy" persona is actively campaigning for the role of Rick according to a memo sent out by Hal Wallis?

5. Ingrid Bergman agreed to the role of Ilsa, in part, because she had initially been turned down for the role of Maria that she really wanted in what film based on a Hemingway novel?

6. The scenes in *Casablanca* of the Moorish (*medina*) Quarter, were adapted from the sets of what film that had recently completed shooting at Warner Bros.?

7. The last character in the film to be shaped into final form and whose character is the biggest change from the play is

_____ .

8. According to the original screen poster or billboard for *Casablanca* the *Mise en Scene* is_____.

9. What studio thought about buying the rights to the play, "Everybody Comes to Rick's" for $5,000, but ultimately rejected the idea?

10. One month after the film is completed, Humphrey Bogart is brought back to dub what Hal Wallis written line?

11. What studio executive of MGM refused to loan Hedy Lamar to Warner Bros. for a screen test for *Casablanca*?

12. What ironic statement does Ilsa say to Rick when he asks if her story has "a wow finish," because Ingrid Bergman has no idea what the finish will be in the film whether she ends up with Rick or Victor?

13. The line "Here's looking at you, kid" is originally what line until Bogart changed it?

14. How much of the $60,000 that Warner Bros. paid to MGM for the services of Ingrid Bergman, did producer David O. Selznick, who owned Bergman's contract, pocket?

15. Renault's line to Rick, after he gets rid of Yvonne, "How extravagant you are, throwing away women like that. Someday they may be scarce," is changed by the Office of War Information from _____ .

16. What is the "war time" reason why the summer shooting day ended at 6:30 PM for *Casablanca*?

17. David O. Selznick recognized the philosophy of Rick as being the same as which character in his most famous production, and continually sent memos to Warner Bros. about how the role should be played?

18. Warner Bros. concentrated their publicity on what film for Best Picture in 1943 instead of *Casablanca*?

19. Bergman did not think about *Casablanca* after being picked to replace dancer Vera Zorina in the role of Maria, in what picture that she really coveted?

20. Although it came in slightly over budget the cost of *Casablanca* is approximately _____ .

21. What producer at MGM wanted to buy the play "Everybody Comes to Rick's" for $5,000, but his bosses did not think it was worth the money?

22. When Warner Bros. attorneys wanted to litigate against the Marx Brothers to keep them from using the name *Casablanca* in their film, *A Night in Casablanca,* Groucho threatened them with litigation of his own by claiming they stole what name from him and Chico, and Harpo, that they had used before the Warner's used it?

23. Instead of starting the writing of *Casablanca* that they were under contract to do, the Epstein Brothers went to Washington, D.C. to work on what award-winning documentary project to explain the war to the troops that is directed by Frank Capra?

24. The two assurances that Paul Henreid got Warner Bros. to agree to before he accepted the role of Victor Laszlo are _____ .

25. What two actors are only seen for five minutes in *Casablanca*, but their roles are memorable ones?

26. *Casablanca* could not be shown in North Africa, even after the allies had taken it over, because the Office of War Information was worried about the sensibilities of the _____ .

27. As a part of the war effort to conserve materials, the movie industries' Film Conservation Committee worked to reduce the use of film by recommending, but not requiring, that each camera set-up have a maximum of how many takes?

28. The most famous "Curtizism" occurred when the director asked for a "poodle" for a shot in the bazaar scene. A prop man found a large black poodle and when he brought it on the set Curtiz bellowed, he did not want a dog but really wanted, as he put it a _____ .

29. Out of the 35 takes of the tarmac scene, sandwiched around hours of arguments between star actor Bogart and director Curtiz, the amount of usable footage for the most memorable scene in film history, is how many seconds?

30. What song is used in the nightclub dance scene, because Warner Bros. owned its rights and could save money by not buying another song?

Answers:

1. **Howard Koch**
2. **Marcel Dalio**
3. **Peter Lorre**
4. **George Raft**
5. *For Whom the Bell Tolls*
6. *The Desert Song*
7. **Ilsa Lund**
8. **Michael Curtiz**
9. **MGM (Metro Goldwyn Mayer)**
10. **"Louis, I think this is the beginning of a beautiful friendship."**
11. **Louis B. Mayer**
12. **"I don't know the finish yet."**
13. **"Here's good luck to you."**
14. **$35,000**
15. **"someday they may be rationed."**
16. **so people could get home before blackout**
17. **Rhett Butler**

18. *Watch on the Rhine*
19. *For Whom the Bell Tolls*
20. 1 million ($1,039,000)
21. Sam Marx
22. Brothers
23. *Why We Fight*
24. equal billing with Bogart and Bergman and he would get the girl in the end
25. Peter Lorre (4) and Sydney Greenstreet (5)
26. Vichy government
27. 3
28. poodle of water (he meant puddle)
29. 39
30. "Perfidia"

Factoid:

Warner Bros. lawyers sent a threatening letter to Groucho Marx while the Marx Brothers were filming, *A Night in Casablanca* in 1946. Groucho wrote back, "I had no idea that the city of Casablanca belonged exclusively to Warner Bros … You probably have the right to use the name Warners, but what about Brothers? Professionally, we were brothers long before you were." A few years later when Warner Bros. announced plans for a biography of Cole Porter to be called *Night and Day,* Groucho Marx threatened a lawsuit of his own saying that it was obvious the studio was infringing on two Marx Brothers' films, *A Night at the Opera* and *A Day at the Races.*

Factoid:

Although he was nominated four times for Best Supporting Actor, Claude Rains never won the Oscar and his failure to win for the role Louis Renault is considered one of the greatest injustices in Academy Award history.

Factoid:

"60 Minutes" commentator Harry Reasoner described *Casablanca* as, "Boy meets girl. Boy loses girl. Boy gets girl back again. Boy gives up girl for humanity's sake."

Factoid:

Many of the 34 nationalities that participated in the making of *Casablanca* were in fact refugees from Europe. This included major stars like Conrad Veidt, Peter Lorre, and Paul Henreid, as well as the numerous bit players who gave the film much of its authenticity.

Factoid:

Canadian ice skater Curt Browning won the Men's World Skating Championship in 1993 by portraying Rick in his routine and skating to the music from *Casablanca*.

Factoid:

When accepting the Academy Award for Best Director, Michael Curtiz, known for his malapropisms, said, "So many times I have a speech ready, but no dice. Always a bridesmaid, never a mother. Now I win, I have no speech."

Factoid:

Leonid Kinskey, who played Sacha the bartender, got his role in the film in replacing Leo Mostovoy by being a drinking buddy of Humphrey Bogart.

"Have you tried twenty-two tonight? I said, twenty-two."

~ Richard Blaine ~

Chapter 28
Numbers

For those interested in numbers *Casablanca* offers up a treasure trove of material. From easy questions like what number does Rick tell Jan to bet? to hard questions like how far are the Germans away from Paris when Rick and Ilsa hear the cannon fire?

Questions:

1. What number does Jan bet on at Rick's suggestion, to win the money for exit visas for himself and Annina?

2. How many times in *Casablanca* does Rick say to Ilsa, "Here's looking at you, kid?"

3. What is Richard Blaine's age in *Casablanca*?

4. What is the table number Rick gives to Victor and Ilsa when they ask for one as close to Sam and as far away from Strasser as possible?

5. How much of the world did Laszlo succeed in impressing according to Rick?

6. What is the number of German couriers who have been shot?

7. The percentage of the profits for Rick's Café Americain that Rick tells Ferrari Sam gets is _____.

8. The number of hours in a day that Strasser wants Laszlo watched is _____.

9. According to Warner Bros., the number of participants of different nationalities that were involved in the making of *Casablanca* is _____.

10. How many days did it take to shoot *Casablanca*?

11. What is the total number of francs the lace seller is trying to sell his tablecloth to Ilsa for, until he finds out she is a "special friend of Rick's?"

12. What is the amount of francs the lace seller is willing to sell his wares to Ilsa for, because she is a "friend" of Rick's?

13. What is the amount of francs the Arab lace seller is willing to sell his wares to Ilsa for because she is a "special friend" of Rick's?

14. What is the type of French drink, named for a French cannon, that the German officer orders for himself and Yvonne?

15. What time in the morning does Jan say he and Annina will meet Renault at Renault's office?

16. What time does Rick say he will meet Ilsa at the train station?

17. In what year did the Americans blunder into Berlin according to Renault?

18. What is the year of the French wine, Veuve Cliquot, that Renault recommends for Strasser to drink at Rick's?

19. In what year did Rick run guns to Ethiopia?

20. In *Casablanca*, what year does Rick mention it is, when he rhetorically asks what time is it in New York?

21. The type of gun that Rick erroneously says the German's are firing as they approach Paris is a _____.

22. In what year did Rick fight on the Loyalist side in Spain?

23. What is the depth of the fog at the airport as expressed in feet?

24. What is the amount of francs on the check that Rick writes "OK" on?

25. How far away are the Germans in miles, according to Rick, as he and Ilsa hear the cannon fire while in Paris?

26. The number of times Rick shoots Major Strasser is _____.

27. The number of days (not including the flashback scene), the action takes place in *Casablanca* is _____.

28. The amount of francs that Rick bets Louis on whether Laszlo will get out of Casablanca or not is _____.

29. The final and highest amount in francs that Rick says he will not accept from Laszlo for the "Letters of Transit" is _____.

30. The amount of money in francs that Rick is to get for Emil from the safe, because someone has won this amount in the casino is _____.

Answers:

1. 22
2. 4
3. 37
4. 30
5. half
6. 2
7. 25
8. 24
9. 34
10. 59
11. 700
12. 200
13. 100
14. 75
15. 6
16. 4:45
17. 1918
18. 26
19. 1935
20. 1941

21. **76**
22. **1936**
23. **500**
24. **1000**
25. **35**
26. **1**
27. **3**
28. **10,000**
29. **3,000,000**
30. **20,000**

Factoid:

The two actors who became refugees and followed the Lisbon trail to the Americas were the husband and wife team of Marcel Dalio (Emil the croupier) and Madeleine LeBeau (Yvonne, Rick's jilted mistress). They left Paris the day before the German's arrived and trekked across Spain to Lisbon; they debarked to Chili, but ended up in Mexico, before going to Canada, and eventually the United States.

Factoid:

For a number of years *Casablanca* was traditionally shown on New Years Eve in Hungary.

Factoid:

The odds of Jan and Annina getting to America were slim. The U.S. quota system established by the Immigration Act of 1924 only allowed 100 Bulgarians a year to enter the United States, and the wait for one of these spots was often many years.

"We'll take the car and drive all night. We'll get drunk. We'll go fishing and stay away until she's gone."

~ Sam ~

Chapter 29
More Numbers

For those who are numerologists, this group of numbers will test your knowledge. Both visual acumen as well as a careful study of dialogue is an essential quality necessary to answer this group of questions.

Questions:

1. The amount of money in francs that Ilsa offers for Rick's thoughts is _____ .

2. The number of minutes before the Lisbon plane is going to take off when Rick, Ilsa, Victor, and Louis arrive at the airport is _____ .

3. The number of days it took to shoot *Casablanca* is _____ .

4. The number of days that *Casablanca* was over schedule when it finished shooting is _____ .

5. The length of the film *Casablanca* in terms of number of minutes is _____ .

6. What is the time that Rick first suggests to Ilsa that he will pick her up to go to the train station?

7. The number of times the man, whose papers had expired, is shot in the opening scene is _____ .

8. The amount of money that the Moor offers the woman for her diamonds, because "diamonds are a drug on the market" is _____ .

9. The amount of francs that Ugarte gets as he cashes in his chips while being arrested is _____ .

10. The amount of francs that the man tells the refugee to bring in order to get on the fishing smack Santiago that leaves from La Medina is _____ .

11. The number of years that Laszlo was in a concentration camp is _____ .

12. The number that is over the arrow of the Paris road sign, as the Germans approach the city is _____ .

13. The number of Academy Awards that *Casablanca* was nominated for is_____.

14. The number of questions that Ilsa says can take care of all of our questions is _____ .

15. The date in December, 1941, when "Everybody Comes to Rick's" title is changed to *Casablanca* is _____ .

16. Renault's starting time for work, the time that he requests Victor and Ilsa meet him at his office is _____ .

17. The approximate number of francs that Jan wins at roulette according to Emil (which is actually an inaccurate figure) is

_____ .

18. When Yvonne asks Sacha for a whole row of French 75s, the German officer actually orders how many?

19. What is the number of times and places that Berger had heard Laszlo had been killed?

20. The amount in cents that Rick's thoughts would bring in America is _____ .

21. The number of shots that Ugarte fires in Rick's Café is _____ .

22. The percent of the profits that Sam actually gets from Rick's Café Americain (although Ferrari says he is worth more) is

_____ .

23. The amount of francs that Laszlo first offers to Rick for the "Letters of Transit" is _____ .

24. The amount in francs that Laszlo raises his offer to when Rick refuses his first offer for the "Letters in Transit" is _____ .

25. The number of *gendarmes* who ride in the car is _____ .

26. The number of miles of visibility in the airport departure scene, before the plane to Lisbon takes off is _____ .

27. The number of francs that Ferrari mentions, when he says not more that this amount to his waiter at the Blue Parrot is

_____ .

28. How many are killed in *Casablanca* either on screen or off screen?

29. What is the phone number of the hospital in Casablanca?

30. What is the phone number of the police station in Casablanca?

Answers:

1. **1**
2. **10**
3. **59**
4. **11**
5. **102**
6. **4:30**
7. **1**
8. **2,400**
9. **2,000**
10. **15,000**
11. **1**
12. **9**
13. **8**
14. **1**
15. **31**
16. **10**
17. **2,000**
18. **2**

19. 5
20. 1
21. 4
22. 10
23. 100,000
24. 200,000
25. 5
26. 1
27. 50
28. 5
29. 713
30. 312

Factoid:

Sidney Greenstreet, who played Ferrari, had made his film debut at the age of 61 playing the fat man, Casper Gutman in *The Maltese Falcon.*

Factoid:

Actor Peter Lorre, who played Ugarte, had been born in the Hungarian part of the old Austro-Hungarian Empire. His birth city is a part of Slovakia today. He was born to Jewish and German parents. This is why his origins have been variously described as German, Austrian, Jewish, and Hungarian.

Factoid:

Because of the success of the film *Algiers*, Jack Warner changed the title of the unproduced stage play "Everybody Comes to Rick's" to *Casablanca.*

"Who knows, in her own way she may constitute an entire second front."

~ Louis Renault ~

Chapter 30
Still More Numbers

The numbers just keep on coming. Raymond Babbit would really be in his element with this group of questions.

Questions:

1. How much money did Rick help Jan win at the roulette table according to the croupier Emil?

2. The 10,000 franc bet that Louis makes with Rick is actually how much money at that time when converted to U.S. dollars?

3. Of the 14 actors who appear in the credits how many were born in the United States?

4. How much did the anonymous Japanese collector pay for Sam's piano that was auctioned off by Sotherby's in 1988?

5. How many of those who were in the cast of *Casablanca* were actual refugees from Europe?

6. *Casablanca* finished in what place at the box office in 1943?

7. In what year is *Casablanca* made?

8. How many francs does Rick first offer to bet Louis regarding Laszlo's escape from Casablanca?

9. Ultimately, how much over budget did *Casablanca* come in at?

10. How much is Humphrey Bogart paid for making *Casablanca*?

11. How many times does Strasser admit that Laszlo slipped through the fingers of the Germans?

12. Compared to Renault's price how much does Ugarte sell exit visas for?

13. Carl tells Rick that they can afford to keep everyone on the payroll while being closed down, for how many weeks?

14. How many weeks ago did the papers expire of the man from the Resistance, who is killed in the opening scene?

15. How many weeks did it take Jan and Annina to travel from Bulgaria to Casablanca?

16. For how long was Laszlo in a German concentration camp?

17. What time does Ilsa agree to meet Rick at the train station?

18. How many bottles of Champagne are Rick, Ilsa, and Sam trying to drink before the Germans get to the café in Paris?

19. How many suitcases combined do Rick and Sam take on the train to Marseilles?

20. The tablecloth the Arab vendor is trying to sell to Ilsa has an initial asking price of how many francs?

21. How many times does Victor kiss Ilsa on the cheek in their hotel room?

22. How many times does Berger say that he read that Laszlo was killed and in how many different places?

23. How many *gendarmes* break into Rick's to arrest Laszlo?

24. How many shots are fired at the man in the opening scene after he runs from the police?

25. How many shots does Ugarte fire in Rick's Café?

26. How many total shots are fired in the film?

27. How much is the Moor willing to pay the woman who is selling her diamonds?

28. How many times does Strasser honk the horn when he is driving to the airport?

29. How many times does the *gendarme* blow the whistle in the opening scene?

30. What number is on the side of the German tank in the Paris newsreel scene?

Answers:

1. **2,000 francs**
2. **$228**
3. **3**
4. **$154,000**
5. **24**
6. **7th**
7. **1942**
8. **20,000**
9. **$75,000**
10. **$36,000**
11. **3**
12. **half (1/2)**
13. **2 or 3**
14. **3**
15. **8**
16. **1**
17. **quarter to five (4:45)**
18. **4**
19. **3**
20. **700**
21. **2**
22. **5**
23. **4**
24. **1**
25. **4**
26. **7**
27. **2,400**
28. **4**

29. 3
30. 105

＊＊＊＊＊＊

Factoid:

In the American Film Institutes' poll of the "Top 100 Movie Lines of All Time," *Casablanca* ranked first with six entries while no other film had more than three. The top ranking and #5 on the list was "Here's looking at you, kid." Also ranked were:

- #20, "Louis, I think this is the beginning of a beautiful friendship;"
- #28, "Play it Sam, play 'As Time Goes By;'"
- #32, "Round up the usual suspects;'
- #43 "We'll always have Paris;" and
- #67, "Of all the gin joints in all the towns in all the world, she walks into mine."

One prominent line that is not listed, which has become a modern metaphor for hypocrisy is Renault's, "I am shocked, shocked to find that gambling is going on in here!" as he collects his winnings.

Factoid:

Instead of "As Time Goes By," the original song written for *Casablanca* that was expected to be the big hit was "Knock on Wood."

Factoid:

When Jack Warner was informed that Humphrey Bogart had been selected as the romantic lead he said, "Who the hell would want to kiss Bogart?"

"What right do I have to think?"

~ Ugarte ~

Chapter 31
Critics & Commentators

Critics, commentators, pundits, and film mavins have had a field day over the years with *Casablanca*. They vie with each other to see who can create the most memorable quote or insight about the film.

There are few films that have had as much said about them as *Casablanca*. Contrary to Ugarte, everyone has the right to think and write about *Casablanca*. Like Notre Dame football and the New York Yankees, *Casablanca* is both loved and hated by its fans and its detractors. The debate goes on, as does *Casablanca*, a tribute to its importance and staying power to our lives.

Questions:

1. What "60 Minutes" commentator described *Casablanca* as, "Boy meets girl. Boy loses girl. Boy gets girl back again. Boy gives up girl for humanity's sake?"

2. What film critic and co-host of "At the Movies," believes the "Key to the movie's drama is Bogart's gradual transition from a man who sticks his neck out for no one to a man who embraces once again the ideals of his youth?"

3. Who allegedly said when he heard Humphrey Bogart had been selected as the romantic lead, "Who in the hell would ever want to kiss Bogart?"

4. What film critic described *Casablanca* as the … "happiest of happy accidents?"

5. What literary figure and critic believes that "*Casablanca* became a cult movie because it is not one movie. It is movies. And this is the reason it works, in defiance of any aesthetic theory?"

6. Manny Farber in his 1942 review for the *New Republic*, panned *Casablanca* by saying "It was as ineffectual" as a short story from what popular magazine?

7. What well-known woman film critic said it was ... "a movie that demonstrates how entertaining a bad movie can be ... ?"

8. After reading the play "Everybody Comes to Rick's," Warner's contract writer Richard Buckner said, "It's big moment is sheer hokum melodrama ... and this guy Rick is two parts Hemingway, one part Scott Fitzgerald and a dash of _____ .

9. Film critic Richard Corliss sees the relationship between Rick and Renault in what type of psychological terms, with Rick as the animus and Renault as the anima?

10. What author of *Round Up the Usual Suspects* describes the film as "A classic movie is the biggest accident of all. A thousand things have to fit together. Fifty years after *Casablanca* was made, I cannot listen to "The Marseilles" drowning out "Watch on the Rhine" without feeling stirred. I cannot watch Bogart and Bergman say goodbye at the airport without feeling the bittersweet tug of lost possibilities?"

11. William Donaldson's "Love and Death in Casablanca," points to Rick rejecting Ilsa and going off with Renault as a case of repressed _____ .

12. What director of *Double Indemnity, Sunset Boulevard,* and *Some Like it Hot,* said *Casablanca* was " ... the most wonderful claptrap that was ever put upon the screen. Claptrap that you can't get out of your mind?"

13. What character does Aljean Harmetz believe is stale and unappealing today, because he lacks ambiguity although ... "he symbolized all that was heroic and noble in an imperfect world?"

14. In 1974, what French "new wave" director said about remaking *Casablanca*, "There can be no doubt that most actors would feel intimidated, as I do and I cannot imagine Jean-Paul Belmondo or Catherine Deneuve being willing to step into the shoes of Humphrey Bogart and Ingrid Bergman?"

15. A studio executive objected to the title of *Casablanca* because it sounded too much like which Mexican beer?

16. In his book, *The Movies of Your Mind*, Harvey Greenberg presents what kind of psychological interpretation that stresses Rick's transgressions that prevent him from returning to the United States as being an Oedipus complex, which is resolved only when Rick begins to identify with the father figure of Laszlo and the cause that he represents?

17. What critic argues that the various names that Rick is called (8 in all) symbolizes the ambiguity that his character represents?

18. In defending the colorization of *Casablanca*, what political commentator said, "Colorization is, in principle, no more than visual dubbing for a generation that is deaf to black and white?"

19. What two-word description did the Directors Guild of America call the colorization of *Casablanca*?

20. What popular TV critic calls *Casablanca*, "The best Hollywood movie of all time?"

21. Leslie Fielder in *Love and Death and the American Novel* compares Rick to *Huckleberry Finn,* the heroes of *Moby Dick,* Hemingway, and James Fenimore Cooper novels in that they make a _____ .

22. Producer Robert Lord categorized the story on the first reading as "A very obvious imitation of _____ ."

23. "... *Casablanca's* (has) unsure standing as a work of art. Unremarkable in 1942, it rose to fame through an accident of timing. No better written or constructed today, it exists primarily as a cultural artifact, a monument of popular culture," according to what critic/commentator?

24. What work by Woody Allen, shows *Casablanca* as a story whose morality, characters, and dialogue can be adapted to social use as icons that transcend their original source?

25. What film critic sees *Casablanca* a half century after its release as the "… apotheosis of the Hollywood romantic melodrama, a kind of fearless and perfected make believe that you probably couldn't get away with today. Singing the Marseilles in the face of the snarling Gestapo. As I am frequently told (as it were somehow my fault) they don't make movies like that any more. It's true, they don't, and I explain sadly that it's because they don't make the world the way they used to, either. Romantic idealism doesn't come as easily as once it did. Information, and rather too much of it, has led us toward being, in Oscar Wilde's formulation, cynics who know the price of everything and the value of nothing …?"

26. The theory about *Casablanca* says that Richard Blaine is FDR, with Victor Laszlo being Churchill, urging him to abandon neutrality is based primarily on the fact that Casablanca in Spanish means _____ .

27. According to what film critic, "If any Hollywood movie exemplifies the "genius of the system," it is surely *Casablanca* – a film whose success was founded on almost as many types of skill as varieties of luck … Mixing genres with mad abandon, *Casablanca* became a cult film … (because) it is 'movies'." All Hollywood movies that is, with a soupcon of the French cinema of the late '30s. In other words, *Casablanca* was the culture of the West, everything we were fighting for in World War II, brought together in one neat package?"

28. "For more than 50 years, *Casablanca* has been over analyzed, overhyped, but certainly not overrated. Its black and white format is more eye catching than even the most colorful of pictures. Elegant, classic, touching, stirring, heartbreaking and romantic are all suitable descriptions …" according to film critic _____ .

29. What critic observed, "*Casablanca* summed up the morality of its time better, I think than any other film ever has … *Casablanca* was how we thought we were, all right, a pure explication of the mood in which we entered World War II and a greater distance than Mars even from the way we eventually came out of it, seduced by power, corrupted by influence?"

It was good to go back again in time to those days when, despite all our faults, we still believed in our own basic virtue?"

30. Jeff Siegel, author of *The Casablanca Companion,* describes *Casablanca* as being a morality play with a view of the world that is as American as the _____ .

Answers:

1. **Harry Reasoner**
2. **Roger Ebert**
3. **Jack Warner**
4. **Andrew Sarris**
5. **Umberto Eco**
6. **Colliers**
7. **Pauline Kael**
8. **café Christ**
9. **Jungian**
10. **Aljean Harmetz**
11. **homosexuality**
12. **Billy Wilder**
13. **Victor Laszlo**
14. **Francois Truffaut**
15. **Carta Blanca**
16. **Freudian**
17. **Sidney Rosenzweig**
18. **Charles Krauthhammer**
19. **artistic desecration**
20. **Leonard Maltin**
21. **flight from society, free from mothers, accompanied by a male companion.**
22. **Grand Hotel**

23. **John Baxter**
24. ***Play It Again Sam***
25. **Charles Champlin**
26. **white house**
27. **J. Hobermain**
28. **David Picup**
29. **Ralph Gleason**
30. **Declaration of Independence**

Factoid:

Although it debuted in November, *Casablanca* was not put into general release until January of 1943. This was so it would not have to compete for the Academy Awards against the popular WWII drama, *Mrs. Minever,* that had been released in December of 1942, and won the Best Picture award for that year.

Factoid:

Rick's Café was modeled after El Minzah Hotel and Café in Tangiers.

Factoid:

During WWII *Casablanca* was banned from being shown in Ireland.

Factoid:

As a soldier in WWI, Claude Rains had been gassed at Vimy Ridge, which almost made him blind in one eye, but he concealed it so well no one knew.

"I'm no good at being noble, but it doesn't take much to see that the problems of three little people don't amount to a hill of beans in this crazy world. Someday you'll understand that. Not now. Here's looking at you, kid."

~ Richard Blaine ~

Chapter 32
Potpourri of
Casablanca Questions

This chapter of 100 questions consists of questions from all 33 categories. Some of them are the most challenging trivia questions in the book.

Questions:

1. Besides Humphrey Bogart, the two actors that are mentioned as possibilities for the lead in the film by the original group of Warner Bros. readers who read the play are _____ .

2. The manuscript of "Everybody Comes to Rick's," reached Warner Bros. studios the day after what historic WWII event?

3. What symbol of the Resistance is found on the papers of the man who has been shot by the police in the opening scene?

4. For what reason is the civilian stopped in the opening scene by the police?

5. At Rick's, what three games are being played?

6. In answer to Strasser's question, what city does Rick say is not particularly his beloved one?

7. The three locations in the film where ceiling fans can be seen are
   _____ .

8. What reason does Carl give for giving Major Strasser the best table, even before he is requested to do so by Captain Renault?

9. To symbolize how insignificant Ugarte is to Rick, during their entire conversation Rick is engaged in what other activity?

10. With news of the murder of the couriers, what three groups or individuals does the pickpocket describe to the English couple as being "rounded up?"

11. What convenient little game does Renault describe to Laszlo regarding his bill at Rick's?

12. What cliché does Sam use when he talks to Ilsa for the first time in Rick's Café, after she says, "Its been a long time?"

13. What is the primary reason that Renault mentions as to why he permits Rick's to stay open?

14. Besides Ilsa, the two characters to kiss Rick in the film are
    _____ .

15. What did Ingrid Bergman say about kissing Humphrey Bogart?

16. What minor character in *Casablanca* wears glasses all the time, not just for reading?

17. What does Rick playfully do with Ilsa, as they are riding the boat on the *Seine* in Paris?

18. What character carries a hat in the film, but never wears it?

19. Because *Casablanca* enhanced her movie career, what other Warner Bros. film, based on an Edna Ferber book, did Ingrid Bergman make for them when she played a courtesan?

20. What character in the film, who appears in the credits, is Islamic in his religious beliefs?

21. Because he "loofs" her, what does Sacha gives Yvonne to drink?

22. What European actress played the women who is selling her jewels in Rick's Café, and is upset by the low price she is offered for them?

23. Who first tells Laszlo that he believes Ugarte left the "Letters of Transit" with Rick?

24. Besides Rick, what eight other names is Rick called by others during the film?

25. The four animals that appear in the film are _____ .

26. What city in Africa does Renault say to Laszlo, he would not leave Ilsa?

27. According to the German's dossier on Rick, his eyes are what color?

28. What is it that Ilsa says to Rick at the linen vendors, that they knew very little about when they were in love in Paris; and if they keep it that way, maybe we'll remember those days and not Casablanca?

29. What does Renault tell his men to do when they search Rick's that would impress the Germans?

30. What two possible reasons does Renault give for Ugarte's death?

31. After Victor and Ilsa leave Renault's office, where does Renault say their next stop will be?

32. What is it that takes the "sting" out of being occupied, according to Sam?

33. What are the last two things that Victor Laszlo says to Rick before he heads for the airplane?

34. What does Ilsa call Rick because he will not sell her the "Letters of Transit?"

35. What does Renault say when Rick tells him the "Letters of Transit" were hidden in Sam's piano?

36. What is the money that Rick wins from Louis Renault on the bet of whether Laszlo will get out of Casablanca, going to be used for?

37. The man who is lamenting that he is "waiting, waiting, waiting," says in despair that he will do what in Casablanca?

38. Because Ingrid Bergman committed adultery in 1949, this star of *Casablanca* became infamous and is condemned by which U.S. government institution?

39. Of all the characters in the film which one is changed the most from the role in the play, "Everybody Comes to Rick's?"

40. What promising actor's career stalled, in part, because of the thankless role he reluctantly took in *Casablanca*?

41. What model is the car that was used to get to the airport, a General Motors product?

42. What type of plane is seen taking off at the end of the film?

43. Because Norway had fought against the Germans when attacked, what two characters in the film are given Norwegian nationalities?

44. Suavity, depravity, and greed under an urbane manner, describes what character?

45. What is the date on the check that Rick writes "OK" on, in the opening scene in his café?

46. What man's signature is necessary on every exit visa of someone leaving Casablanca?

47. The reason Strasser gives for having Rick's closed down is because everyone is having _____ .

48. When Victor and Ilsa go to Renault's office, what two minor characters are in the lobby talking to a *gendarme* who cannot help them?

49. When Renault is comparing himself to Rick, he says you are the only one in Casablanca who has less of what desirable quality than I do?

50. In one sense, the role of Renault played by Hector Elizondo in the 1983 TV version is more realistic than the Claude Rains role, because, unlike Rains, he plays the character with a _____ .

51. The three character actors in *Casablanca* who were also in the 1955 TV version are _____ .

52. A postcard sold for $1,750 that had 14-P-Q5 written on it from Humphrey Bogart during the filming of *Casablanca*. What did the letters and numbers stand for on the postcard?

53. How is Irving Kovner related to the making of the film *Casablanca*?

54. What is Rick doing when Renault says, "Now you are beginning to live like a Frenchman?"

55. As the two *gendarmes* approach Ugarte to arrest him in Rick's, how do they address him?

56. What facial feature does the Arab lace seller have, that no other member of the cast with a speaking part has?

57. What seems to be the flower of choice in *Casablanca*, because at various times Rick, Strasser, and the German banker are seen wearing it?

58. What gesture of toughness does Renault demonstrate, when he tells Rick "In Casablanca I am the master of my fate?"

59. In the opening scene what activity is the man doing in the street that is rather unusual?

60. What type of boat is leaving Casablanca at 1:00 AM in he morning?

61. What is Rick doing when he first sees Ilsa and Victor come into his café the second night?

62. What is it that Rick got stuck with that entitles him to know why Ilsa ran out on him in Paris?

63. In order to get two exit visas from Renault what is it that is implied (because of the censors) that Annina will have to do?

64. What is the name of the newspaper that has news of the Germans entering Paris, that Ilsa and Rick are reading at the *Café Pierre*?

65. What is in the container on the desk of the officer who is reading the announcement regarding the murder of the German couriers?

66. What physical action does Rick do right before he says, "Of all the gin joints in all the towns in all the world, she walks into mine!"

67. According to Carl, the father of the leading banker in Amsterdam has what job at Rick's Café?

68. What continent is shown in the opening scenes with the credits superimposed on it?

69. What five letters are on the plane that arrives in the opening scene?

70. While Rick and Louis are talking outside the café, what is coming from the airport to illuminate their conversation?

71. Which employee of Rick's owes what other employee money?

72. What is Carl physically doing when patrons of the casino – who had witnessed the incident with Jan at the roulette table – ask him, "Is this place honest?"

73. What is at both ends of Corina's guitar that fits in with the Moroccan décor and architecture?

74. What does Renault do to get ready to see a young lady, after telling the officer to "send her in" when he has been informed that there is another visa problem?

75. 1/4 oz. lemon juice, a dash of sugar syrup, a dash of grenadine, 3/4 oz. gin over ice cubes in a shaker, strain into a champagne flute, and fill with champagne is a recipe for what type of drink served at Rick's?

76. Heinze's official job and title in *Casablanca* is _____ .

77. For most people who enjoy the artistry of the cinematography in *Casablanca*, what did Ted Turner do to the film in 1987 that caused outrage?

78. The arbitrary element in the plot – that is sometimes called a McGuffin – because it makes no logical sense, but is used to motivate the action, is the _____ .

79. According to Carl, in his conversation with the women playing baccarat, the leading banker from Amsterdam has what job in Rick's kitchen?

80. What is Rick's term (borrowed from Ferrari) for the incidental expenses that Ferrari will charge for handling the disposition of the "Letters of Transit?"

81. When Rick puts Yvonne in a taxi, the censors changed Renault's line in Casablanca regarding throwing away women to "Someday they may be scarce," from "Someday they may be _____ ."

82. Ferrari believes that Rick is a difficult customer because "One never knows what he _____ ."

83. The montage of war-time documentary footage in the credits scene, and Germans approaching Paris in the flashback scene, are both by _____ .

84. When the band plays "Knock on Wood" every time the lyric knock on wood is sung they _____ .

85. Producer Hal Wallis was deprived of the opportunity to collect the Academy Award for Best Picture because what studio executive beat him to the podium to collect the award?

86. What science fiction novella in the series, *The Man-Kzin Wars,* created and edited by Larry Niven, has a plot that draws many elements from *Casablanca*?

87. Neo-noir film of 1995, whose screenplay by Christopher McQuarrie won an Academy Award, uses what line from Louis Renault in *Casablanca* as its title?

88. On April 26, 1943, what 30-minute radio program presented an adaptation of *Casablanca* starring Humphrey Bogart, Ingrid Bergman, and Paul Henreid?

89. It has been reported that what Bollywood director is going to do a Malaysian language remake of *Casablanca*, set in southern India, and revolving around the Tamil's conflict with the Sinhalese civil government in Sri Lanka?

90. One reason why the other proposed ending of Rick and Ilsa going off together would never have happened, is because a married woman leaving her husband for another man would have been forbidden by the _____ .

91. Regarding Ted Turner's colorization of *Casablanca*, Humphrey Bogart's son Stephen stated that if you are going to colorize *Casablanca,* you might as well put arms on the _____ .

92. What 1980's TV program parodied *Casablanca* in one episode starring Curtis Armstrong as Rick and Alyce Beasley as Ilsa?

93. The song recorded by Dooley Wilson that is written for *Casablanca*, but cut from the film is _____ .

94. Humphrey Bogart (Rick), Sydney Greenstreet (Ferrari), John Qualen (Berger), S.Z. Sakall (Carl) are all buried in what cemetery in Glendale, California?

95. What recent film reproduces many elements of the *Casablanca* movie poster, including the "stacked heads" cast gallery and the brush hand-lettering style title treatment?

96. What reason does Berger give on how he is able to recognize Victor Laszlo at Rick's?

97. What is superimposed on the screen as the narrator describes the refugee trail that goes across the Mediterranean from Europe to Africa?

98. What does Rick say Casablanca is a good spot for doing?

99. How much did the tickets cost at the Hollywood Theatre in New York City for the premiere showing of the film?

100. The name chosen for the Prefect of Police, Louis Renault, by the Epstein's, is picked for what practical reason?

Answers:

1. James Cagney and George Raft
2. Pearl Harbor
3. Cross of Lorraine
4. To see his papers
5. Baccarat, chess, roulette
6. Paris
7. Blue Parrot, Renault's office, and Rick's Café
8. "He is German and would take it anyway."
9. playing chess
10. "refugees, liberals, and a beautiful young girl for the Prefect of Police"
11. "they put it on the bill, I tear up the bill"
12. "a lot of water under the bridge"
13. Rick has never sold an exit visa.
14. Sacha and Annina (Bulgarian girl)
15. "I kissed him but I never knew him."
16. Heinze
17. tosses her a peanut (nut)
18. Ugarte
19. Saratoga Trunk
20. Ferrari
21. "bosse's private stock" (alcohol)
22. Lotte Palfi
23. Ferrari
24. Boss, Monsieur Blaine, Mr. Richard, Richard, Mr. Rick, Ricky, Herr Rick, darling (by Ilsa)
25. monkey, dog, horses, parrot
26. Oran
27. brown
28. each other
29. "be especially destructive"
30. committed suicide or died trying to escape
31. black market
32. drinking champagne
33. "And welcome back to the fight. This time I know our side will win."
34. "a coward and a weakling"
35. "Serves me right for not being musical."
36. Rick and Louis' expenses to the Free French garrison at Brazzaville
37. die
38. U.S. Senate
39. Ilsa Lund
40. Paul Henreid
41. Buick
42. Lockheed Electra 12A
43. Ilsa Lund & Berger
44. Ferrari
45. 2 December, 1941
46. Renault
47. "much too good a time"
48. Jan and Annina Brandel
49. scruples
50. French accent
51. Dan Seymour, Marcel Dalio, Ludwig Stossel
52. his chess moves
53. he is the one playing chess by mail with Bogart
54. having a drink
55. monsieur Ugarte
56. beard

57. carnation
58. puts his thumbs in his belt
59. juggling
60. smack (ketch)
61. checking the reservation list
62. railway ticket
63. have sex with Renault
64. Paris Soir
65. 3 pencils
66. pounds the table
67. bellboy
68. Africa
69. DAGOF
70. searchlight
71. Carl owes Sacha
72. polishing a platter
73. tassels
74. checks himself in the mirror and straightens his tie
75. French 75's
76. German Consul
77. colorized it
78. "Letters of Transit"
79. pastry chef

80. carrying charges
81. rationed
82. what he'll do or why
83. Don Siegel and James Leicester
84. knock on their checks
85. Jack Warner
86. "The Children's Hour"
87. *The Usual Suspects*
88. Screen Guild Theatre
89. Rajeev Nath
90. Breen Production Code
91. Venus di Milo
92. "Moonlighting"
93. "Dat's What Noah Done"
94. Forest Lawn
95. *The Good German*
96. news photographs
97. ships
98. dying
99. 40 cents
100. It was the name of a French car that Americans were familiar with.

Factoid:

Two of the most memorable roles in film are by Peter Lorre as Ugarte and Sidney Greenstreet as Ferrari, and both actors' roles had only about five minutes of screen time.

Factoid:

Instead of *Casablanca*, Ingrid Bergman is nominated for Best Actress in 1943 for the role of Maria in *For Whom the Bell Tolls.*

"Louis, I think this is the beginning of a beautiful friendship."
~ Richard Blaine ~

Chapter 33
More Potpourri

Many in this group of questions are truly for the *aficionado*; others are just commonplace leftovers from the previous 32 chapters/ categories. For those who have seen *Casablanca* a number of times, or have read any of the books written about the film, many of these questions are for you. *"More Potpourri"* concludes the 1,130 trivia questions contained in *"Casablanca Film Trivia: Here's Looking at You, Kid."*

Questions:

1. Warner Bros. studio executive Steve Trilling had what minor Arab character with a speaking part eliminated in order to save money?

2. In addition to George Raft, what other actor under contract to Warner Bros., is mentioned as a possibility for the lead by the early readers of the play?

3. What nationality is Paul Henreid originally, although he became a German when they marched in and took over his country?

4. What Warner Bros. expenditure of $4,133 is wasted, because what it is spent on was not used in the film?

5. The role of Lois Meredith, an American character in the play, is changed to the role of what European character in the film?

6. After the top three stars, what four actors received equal supporting role billing?

7. What office or title does Louis Renault hold?

8. The character played by Ingrid Bergman used her maiden name in the film, but her married name in the film is actually _____ .

9. What is significant about August 3rd, 1942 regarding *Casablanca*?

10. Ingrid Bergman's services in *Casablanca* for eight weeks were traded by MGM for the services of what Warner Bros. actress?

11. Of the four main characters in *Casablanca*, which one remains essentially the same as the one in the stage play?

12. What character is a charming, womanizing, amoral chief of police?

13. "Star-crossed lovers who play out a bittersweet tale of romance found, lost, rekindled, and sacrificed" describes what two characters in the film?

14. Rick tells Renault that the reason he came to Casablanca is for his _____ .

15. Because of production delays, what actor's salary went way over budget as his five minutes of screen time stretched over many weeks?

16. The four actors from *Casablanca* who also starred in *Passage to Marseilles* are _____ .

17. What two characters, because their names, were intended to be of Italian background, are given only surnames in the film?

18. The writer/director Robert Rossen called "Everybody Comes to Rick's" a piece of _____ .

19. What character actor was hired for $3,750 a week for five minutes work in the film, and was ultimately paid for eight weeks work?

20. Instead of *Casablanca*, what role, and in what film, is Ingrid Bergman nominated Best Actress in 1943?

21. What two actors never see each other during the filming, as one finishes his scenes before the other arrives to do his?

22. What minor character, the German Consul, is the first to greet Strasser as he gets off of the plane?

23. Until Leonid Kinskey got the role, the name of the Russian bartender is not Sacha, but _____ .

24. Instead of ordering Victor Laszlo and Ilsa to come to his office, what does Renault do that is a much more pleasant word?

25. Corpulent, jovial, German waiter/bookkeeper describes what character?

26. A humorous, demonstrative, love sick Russian, describes what character?

27. The three characters who attend the meeting of the Resistance are _____ .

28. Who is it that Rick says someday Ilsa will lie to?

29. As Ferrari laments about the death of Ugarte, Rick calls Ferrari what pejorative term?

30. The main reason Ferrari is upset because Ugarte is dead, is because no one knows where the _____ .

31. What performer in *Casablanca*, who is nominated for an Academy Award for Supporting Actor, claimed that he had never seen the film?

32. Instead of being able to collect the Oscar for Best Picture, what Honorary Academy Award did producer Hal Wallis receive in 1943?

33. When *Casablanca* won the Academy Award for Best Picture, who stepped up to receive the Oscar that caused a irreparable rift with producer Hal Wallis, who thought he should have been the one to receive the award?

34. Two days before the Academy Award ceremonies, in which he was nominated for Best Actor for *Casablanca*, Bogart started work on what picture that had similarities to *Casablanca*?

35. Humphrey Bogart lost the Academy Award for Best Actor in 1943 to what actor for his role in *Watch on the Rhine*?

36. What character, who is loved by one of Rick's employees, is Rick's jilted mistress?

37. What is Strasser's military rank?

38. The important guest that Renault tells Rick will be at his café, is a Major in what European government?

39. What destination is the ultimate goal of Victor and Ilsa?

40. Renault's remark "I don't interfere with them and they don't interfere with me" is a reference to the _____ .

41. The line "Here's looking at you, kid" is originally what line until Bogart changed it?

42. How does Renault describe the woman he is going to be coming into Rick's with the next night, that he wants her to lose at gambling?

43. Although he is never seen with a woman, the four women in *Casablanca* that Renault shows a sexual interest in are

_____ .

44. Renault tells Strasser that Rick is completely neutral about everything, and that takes into account what field too?

45. Although the fortunate ones obtain exit visas and scurry to Lisbon and the New World, what do the others do in Casablanca?

46. How do Rick, Ilsa, and Victor address Ferrari that indicates his nationality?

47. In what country did the release of *Casablanca* fail to be a hit during the post WWII period, in part, because of its depiction of Vichy, but later it became a hit?

48. What is superimposed on the long shot of the revolving globe in the opening shot of the film?

49. With the coming of the second World War, many eyes in imprisoned Europe turned hopefully or desperately toward the freedom of the _____ .

50. After calling the German who came in with Yvonne the second night a derogatory name, what else does the French officer say that he will get someday?

51. What does Rick do during the singing of "Knock on Wood," that someone should have noticed, but no one did?

52. In the café scene the second night, what song did the Germans originally sing, but it had to be replaced because it was under copyright protection from Germany?

53. What creative force is the highest paid at $73,000?

54. What actor was paid $5,000 a week, that made him the highest paid actor in the film on a weekly basis?

55. Opportunistic café owner and black marketer describes what character?

56. Who received a salary of $52,000 for making *Casablanca*?

57. What is the eight-word prepositional phrase that begins the film?

58. What two individuals originally optioned the play, "Everybody Comes to Rick's" for production?

59. What character in the film got his role because he was an actual drinking buddy of Bogart's?

60. What actor finished his role in *Now Voyager* on June 3rd and did his first scene for *Casablanca* on June 4th?

61. The three character actors in *Casablanca* who starred in the 1955 TV version are _____ .

62. The two songs in the film that call for general audience participation are _____ .

63. The subtle film composers art, which Max Steiner excelled at in *Casablanca*, of linking a bit of music to an on screen action or character reference, is called what term named for a cartoon character?

64. What actress, working on her first film, is paid $100 a week and guaranteed two weeks, but ended up working eight weeks because her scenes were delayed?

65. In 1991, Murray Burnett, the writer of the play that *Casablanca* is based on, rewrote it as two acts and renamed it from "Everybody Comes to Rick's" to _____ .

66. Julius Epstein said that *Casablanca* had more of what product than the states of Kansas and Iowa combined?

67. Frank Puglia is the actor who played what character?

68. The three methods of transportation mentioned by the narrator to get from Oran to Casablanca are _____ .

69. Who is Strasser calling on the phone while he is shot by Rick?

70. Rick tells Laszlo on the tarmac that Ilsa came to his apartment and tried everything to get what from him the night before?

71. What is Rick referring to when he says to Laszlo,"Keep it. You'll need it in America?"

72. Instead of calling the airport as he says he is doing at Rick's, Renault calls _____ .

73. Specifically, where does Victor Laszlo have a scar?

74. At the airport, what is it that Renault tells Rick he is going to have to do, that will not be very pleasant for either of them, especially Rick?

75. Rick tells Ilsa on the tarmac that nine chances out of 10, they would both end up where if she stayed in Casablanca with him?

76. After commenting that Germany would be grateful if Laszlo was put in a concentration camp, Renault corrects himself by saying who would be very grateful?

77. Renault says he is going to miss Rick, because Rick is apparently the only one in Casablanca with less of what admirable quality than Renault has?

78. When Laszlo is discussing destiny with Rick, and the *gendarmes* come in and arrest Laszlo, what does Rick say in response to this action?

79. What does Sam say he is playing on the piano when Rick asks him to "play it" "As Time Goes By?"

80. After selling his club to Ferrari, what does Rick say he has already talked to Ferrari about, to reassure Renault?

81. When Rick and Ilsa are at the *Café Pierre,* Rick asks Ilsa to translate the announcement being made over the loudspeakers because his _____ .

82. According to Rick, what will Laszlo do in Casablanca that Rick will also do because it is a good place for it?

83. When Ilsa calls Rick, "Richard," in *Casablanca*, what is Rick's reply?

84. What does Carl offer to give Laszlo, after they have escaped from the underground meeting and come into Rick's with Laszlo's injury?

85. What is the reason why Rick tells Ilsa not to bring up Paris?

86. What does Strasser tell Ilsa, after the closing of Rick's Cafe, that the French authorities might do to Laszlo?

87. What geographic problem of seating does Rick have to solve when Victor and Ilsa come in to his café the second night?

88. What does Renault say he has to do to Strasser, after he and Rick conclude their conversation regarding the "Letters of Transit" the second night?

89. What is Strasser referring to when he says it is honeycombed with traitors waiting for their chance?

90. Who is Annina (Bulgarian girl) referring to when she says, "... He is so kind. He wants to help us?"

91. What reason does Rick give to Laszlo, for not selling him the "Letters of Transit" for any price?

92. What does Renault accuse Rick of being, for helping Jan and Annina by letting Jan win at roulette?

93. Throughout the film, what does Rick say his profession is?

94. When Ilsa is berating Rick for wanting to feel sorry for himself, and thinking of only his own feelings, what two words does she call him?

95. What is Ilsa's response to Rick's series of questions:
   • "Who are you really?";
   • "What did you do before?";
   • "What did you do?"; and
   • "What did you think?"

96. In return for sexual favors, what is Renault willing to give to Annina even though she has no money?

97. What is it that is so expensive and difficult and cost Jan and Annina much more than they thought it would?

98. What film critic has called the Paul Henreid character a pig?

99. What two reasons does Renault give for helping Victor and Ilsa by calling them a taxi the first night at Rick's Café?

100. After selling his café to Ferrari, what does Rick remind Ferrari that he owes to Rick's?

Answers:

1. Muezzin
2. James Cagney
3. Austrian
4. Script of MacKenzie & Klein
5. Ilsa Lund
6. Conrad Veidt, Claude Rains, Peter Lorre, and Sydney Greenstreet
7. Prefect of Police
8. Ilsa Laszlo
9. The day it finished shooting.
10. Olivia de Havilland
11. Victor Laszlo
12. Louis Renault
13. Rick & Ilsa
14. Health
15. Sydney Greenstreet
16. Bogart, Lorre, Greenstreet, Rains
17. Ugarte and Ferrari
18. crap
19. Sydney Greenstreet
20. Maria in *For Whom the Bell Tolls*
21. Peter Lorre & Paul Henreid
22. Heinze
23. Fydor
24. request
25. Carl
26. Sacha
27. Lazlo, Carl, Berger
28. Victor Laszlo
29. A fat hypocrite
30. "Letters of Transit" are.
31. Claude Rains
32. Irving Thalberg
33. Jack Warner
34. *To Have and Have Not*
35. Paul Lucas
36. Yvonne
37. Major
38. Third Reich
39. America
40. Gestapo
41. "Here's good luck to you"
42. breath taking blonde
43. Ilsa, Yvonne, Annina (Bulgarian girl), and the breathtaking blonde
44. women
45. wait
46. Signor
47. France
48. refugees
49. Americas
50. revenge
51. Hides the "Letters of Transit" in Sam's piano.
52. "Horst Wessel"
53. Director Michael Curtiz
54. Sydney Greenstreet
55. Ferrari
56. Producer Hal Wallis
57. "With the coming of the Second World War ..."
58. Martin Gabel & Carly Wharton
59. Sacha
60. Claude Rains
61. Dan Seymour, Marcel Dalio, Ludwig Stossel

62. "Knock on Wood" and *"Marseilles"*
63. "Mickey Mousing"
64. Joy Page
65. "Rick's Bar Casablanca"
66. corn
67. Arab vendor or lace seller
68. auto, train, foot
69. the radio tower
70. "Letters of Transit"
71. The money for the "Letters of Transit."
72. Major Strasser
73. above his right eyebrow
74. arrest him
75. concentration camp
76. Vichy
77. scruples
78. destiny has taken a hand
79. something of my own
80. he will still win at roulette
81. German's a little rusty
82. die
83. Were back in Paris.
84. water
85. it is poor salesmanship
86. find a reason to put him in a concentration camp
87. a table close to Sam and as far away from Strasser as possible
88. flatter him
89. every French province
90. Renault
91. Ilsa (ask your wife)
92. a rank sentimentalist
93. saloon keeper
94. coward and weakling
95. "We said, no questions."
96. exit visas
97. traveling
98. Roger Ebert
99. gasoline rationing and time of night
100. 100 cartons of American cigarettes

Factoid:

He first became a star for his role in *The Maltese Falcon*, but after *Casablanca*, Humphrey Bogart replaced Errol Flynn as the #1 star for Warner Bros.

Factoid:

Ceiling fans figure prominently in the film at Rick's Café, the police station, and the Blue Parrot.

~ *Notes* ~

~ Notes ~

Bibliography

Anobile, Richard, ed. *Casablanca*. New York: Darien House, Inc., 1974

Cahill, Marie. Hollywood Classics: *Casablanca*. New York: Smithmark Publishers, 1991.

Francisco, Charles. *You Must Remember This: The Filming of Casablanca.* Englewood Cliffs, New Jersey: Prentice-Hall, 1980.

Harmetz, Aljean. *Round Up the Usual Suspects: The Making of Casablanca—Bogart, Bergman, and World War II.* New York: Hyperion, 1992.

Koch, Howard. *Casablanca: Script and Legend.* Woodstock, New York: The Overlook Press, 1992.

Lebo, Harlan, *Casablanca: Behind the Scenes.* New York: Simon and Schuster, 1992.

Miller, Frank. *Casablanca: As Time Goes By* (50th Anniversary Commemorative). Atlanta: Turner Publishing Inc., 1997.

Osborne, Richard E. *The Casablanca Companion: The Movie Classic and It's Place in History.* Indianapolis: Riebel-Roque Publishing Company, 1997.

Siegel, Jeff. *The Casablanca Companion: The Behind the Scenes Story of an American Classic.* Dallas: Taylor Publishing Company, 1992

~ Notes ~